Kabbalah and Meditation
for the Nations

THE TEACHINGS OF KABBALAH SERIES

by Rabbi Yitzchak Ginsburgh

The Hebrew Letters
Channels of Creative Consciousness

The Mystery of Marriage
How to Find True Love and Happiness in Married Life

Awakening the Spark Within
Five Dynamics of Leadership that can Change the World

Transforming Darkness into Light
Kabbalah and Psychology

Rectifying the State of Israel
A Political Platform based on Kabbalah

Living in Divine Space
Kabbalah and Meditation

Body, Mind, and Soul
Kabbalah on Human Physiology, Disease, and Healing

Consciousness & Choice
Finding Your Soulmate

The Art of Education
Internalizing Ever-New Horizons

What You Need to Know About Kabbalah

Kabbalah and Meditation for the Nations

Anatomy of the Soul

A Sense of the Supernatural
Interpretation of Dreams and Paranormal Experiences

Kabbalah and Meditation for the Nations

Rabbi Yitzchak Ginsburgh

Edited by Rabbi Moshe Genuth

Gal Einai

Jerusalem • New York • Los Angeles

THE TEACHINGS OF KABBALAH SERIES

KABBALAH AND MEDITATION FOR THE NATIONS

Rabbi Yitzchak Ginsburgh

Edited by Rabbi Moshe Genuth

Printed in the United States of America and Israel
First Edition

FOR INFORMATION:

Israel: GAL EINAI
         PO Box 1015
         Kfar Chabad 72915
         tel. (in Israel): 1-700-700-966
         tel. (from abroad): 972-3-9608008
email: books@inner.org

Web: www.inner.org

GAL EINAI produces and publishes books, pamphlets, and recorded
lectures by Rabbi Yitzchak Ginsburgh. To receive a catalog of our
products in English and/or Hebrew, please contact us at any of the
above addresses, email ge@inner.org, or visit our website.

Text Layout: David Hillel

Cover Design: Shmuel Kaffe

ISBN: 978-965-7146-12-5

Table of Contents

Editor's Note

Rabbi Israel Ba'al Shem Tov, the founder of the Chassidic movement which brought about a renaissance in Jewish spirituality starting some 300 years ago, said that the Laws of *Bnei Noach* create a bond of responsibility between the Jewish people and the nations of the world.

In our own times, the Lubavitcher Rebbe brought the Laws of *Bnei Noach* to the forefront of our efforts to bring lasting peace and prosperity to the Jewish people and the entire world. Time and again, the Rebbe explained that the world is ready to accept responsibility for these laws and to renew the covenant made between Noah and the Almighty after the Flood, as recounted in Genesis.

The Laws of *Bnei Noach* are not another religion that Jews would like to encourage non-Jews to accept. In fact, they are not a religion at all. Rather, they are the framework for creating a better world, a better humanity, based on the bond that every human being can enjoy with his or her Creator.

Though technical at first glance, overall the Noahide covenant is based on principles whose value and importance in creating a just and moral society are easily recognized by most, if not all people in the world today. But, the principles of the Laws of *Bnei Noach* are different than any rational set of laws that could be legislated by any court of law today, for they were legislated by the Creator Himself and given to us as the basis for His relationship with humanity as a whole.

There is no question that the world is now experiencing a religious revival. This revival, though positive in some aspects, is bringing about what some call a clash of civilizations whose end cannot be foreseen. Instead of encouraging peace, understanding, and tolerance, the respective commitments to the Creator of both Christians and Moslems alike are threatening to cause terrible turmoil. This is exactly the time for the Jewish people to fulfill their mission as God's chosen people and together with the non-Jews who have already embraced and committed themselves to the Laws of *Bnei Noach* to spread the message of these laws and offer hope, in the form of a truly universal covenant between man and God, for a new era that can dawn upon us all.

The Lubavitcher Rebbe impressed upon his Jewish brothers and sisters the need to make sincere inroads to the hearts of non-Jews and to be receptive to their spiritual needs. Thus, most Chabad-Lubavitch centers are willing to teach non-Jews how to be *Bnei Noach* either directly or by referring them to their local appropriate Torah authority.

According to the Lubavitcher Rebbe, bringing the seven Laws of *Bnei Noach* to the non-Jewish world is a most worthy endeavor for all Jews. In a letter, the Rebbe wrote:

> "...Chassidut contains teachings not only for the Jewish people, but for non-Jews, as well, inasmuch as the seven commandments of *Bnei Noach* are also expounded upon and explained in Chassidut in novel, mystical and lucid perspectives, shedding light on all their aspects...."

Indeed, because the recent religious revival has taken on a predominantly spiritual nature, we feel that there is special room and need for this volume about the Noahide covenant. Rabbi Ginsburgh's unique gift that he has shared over the years with all of us is his singular mastery of the mystical-spiritual tradition of the Torah. Thus, this book takes a unique perspective on the Laws of *Bnei Noach* and seeks to reveal the depth of their mystical secrets and spiritual guidance. In that respect, we recognize that this book occupies a special niche and it is our hope that it will contribute to the growth of the *Bnei Noach* movement.

The contents of this present volume were produced over the last 10 years. Most of the material found in chapters 1, 3, and 7 was developed specifically for this book. Chapter 2 originally appeared as a pamphlet titled "True Monotheism," which was written as a response to Christian missionary activity. Some of chapter 3 and almost all of chapter 4 appeared in the past as a pamphlet titled "The Seven Principles of Divine Service for Righteous Gentiles." Chapter 5 is made up of various responses to questions posed to Rabbi Ginsburgh through Gal Einai's website (www.inner.org). Finally, the contents of chapter 6 were written as background material that was handed out to Christian tourists to the Land of Israel in the year 2000, as well as a call to the religious leaders of the world in lieu of the Pope's visit to the Holy Land in that same year.

In this volume we have followed the same conventions as those used in past volumes. A particularly useful survey of these conventions can be found in *The Mystery of Marriage*. We briefly mention only that when "GOD" (in small-caps) appears in a quote it is in specific reference to His essential Name, *Havayah* (i.e., the Tetragrammaton). Otherwise, "God" can refer to any of the sanctified Names of the Almighty, a discussion of which, along with many other newer conventions, can be found in our last volume *What You Need to Know About Kabbalah*.

We would like to take this opportunity to acknowledge the contributions of all those whose time and effort went into preparing this book. They include Yechezkel Anis, Rabbi Asher and Mrs. Sarah Esther Crispe, Mrs. Uriela Sagiv, and Rabbi Moshe Wisnefsky.

Moshe Genuth
16th of Cheshvan, 5767
Toronto, Canada

Introduction

The Crown Jewels

Arguably, the 10 Commandments are the most famous religious document in the world. Actually, calling them the 10 Commandments is an incorrect translation of their Hebrew name, which would more correctly be translated as the Ten Articles (*Aseret Hadibrot,* in Hebrew).[1] Though they are made up of 10 separate articles, they include more than 10 of the Torah's 613 commandments. Indeed, even the earliest commentators on the Torah write that the text of the Ten Commandments alludes to all 613 commandments.[2] The most important allusion to this is that the original Hebrew text of the Ten Commandments (as they appear in Exodus 20:2 thru 20:13) contains exactly 620 letters. 620 is 7 more than 613. According to some Rabbinic authorities,[3] the 7 commandments that complement the 613 commandments given to the Jewish people are the 7 Laws of *Bnei Noach,* that were given to the first generations of man, beginning with Adam.

620 is the numerical value of the word "crown," in Hebrew. As such we find that the Jewish people—who carry the responsibility for 613 commandments—together with the righteous gentiles who are responsible for the universal commandments, together adorn the Almighty's crown of

Kingship over the entire world with 620 jewels—the commandments of the Almighty's words unto man.

God's Universal Instructions

The Torah portion that is most associated with righteous gentiles is Noah.[4] It begins with the Torah describing Noah's character: "Noah was a righteous and earnest man among the people of his time, and he walked with God."[5] Every non-Jew who wishes to walk with God[6] should seek to emulate Noah, who through his commitment to follow the word of God, saved the human race from extinction during the Flood. As the Torah relates:

> The earth was corrupt before God, and the earth was filled with violence. And God saw the earth and beheld that it was corrupt, for all flesh had corrupted its way on the earth. And God said to Noah, "The end of all flesh has come. The earth is filled with violence because of them, and so, I will destroy them with the earth...."[7]

When Noah and his family emerged from the Ark they had built, God formed a new covenant with them, and hence with all of humanity.[8] He blessed Noah and his family and instructed them in the ways of the new order, declaring:

> "I have now given you everything.... And thus, of the blood of your souls, I will demand an account...."[9]

God's instructions to Noah, who became the progenitor of all those born after the Flood, are binding on all human beings— "the children of Noah," or *Bnei Noach* in Hebrew. These instructions (most of which were given earlier to Adam[10]) are broken down into seven general commandments known today as the seven Laws of *Bnei Noach*. They are:

- a prohibition against worshiping any entity other than the One God,
- a prohibition against blaspheming God's Name,
- a prohibition against murder,
- a prohibition against theft,
- a prohibition against adultery,
- a prohibition against eating the flesh of a live animal,
- a proscription to establish a court system to ensure a just society based on these laws.[11]

The Significance of Divine Instructions

To understand the full significance of these seven laws one must first recognize that the Torah (i.e., the Five Books of Moses) is not merely a book of stories about the first few generations of mankind, the Children of Israel, their exodus from Egypt, and their wanderings in the desert. The Torah is also more than a legal document listing the commandments prescribed by the Creator. More comprehensively, the Torah is and should be experienced as a revelation of God Himself— particularly of His Will. In the language of the *Zohar*, "God and the Torah are one."[12]

As a revelation of the Almighty's Will, the Torah can be described as a user's manual for life, revealing to those who study it the manufacturer's operating instructions. Considering this, the Laws of *Bnei Noach* cannot be viewed as merely technical requirements God makes of human beings.

Instead they are the very revelation of God's Will. By committing to keeping these commandments a person is already manifesting the Will of the Almighty in our mundane reality. All of God's expectations of what we as human beings, as His creations, can achieve operationally depend and practically pass through the acceptance and commitment to practicing the seven Laws of *Bnei Noach*. Moreover, as manifestation of the Divine Will these seven laws are actually part of the mechanisms of the universe—the light, energy, and forces that make the universe function.

Getting the Message Out

Subsequent to His covenant with Noah, God made a covenant with Abraham,[13] and with Abraham's son Isaac, and with his grandson Jacob,[14] to whom God gave the name "Israel."[15] At Mt. Sinai, "the children of Israel," *Bnei Yisrael* in Hebrew, experienced *en masse* a revelation of the Almighty and were given the Torah (the Five Books of Moses),[16] with laws comprising 613 commandments.[17] These 613 commandments are binding only upon *Bnei Yisrael* (the Jewish people), and it is through these commandments that Jews fulfill their special mission in the world.

The Torah is replete with verses[18] clearly stating that the Jewish people were chosen by God to fill a special role. For example:

> "Now therefore, if you will obey My voice and keep My covenant, then you shall be My own treasure among all peoples; for all the earth is Mine; And you shall be to Me a kingdom of priests and a holy nation."[19]

As a result of this special assignment from God, the Jews have a responsibility to be a "light unto the nations"[20] — this means that they are responsible to teach non-Jews how to obey the seven Laws of *Bnei Noach* and by doing so to lead the entire world to the true worship of the One God, thus bringing about the final redemption, as Isaiah prophesized:

> In the days to come, the Mount of GOD's House shall stand firm above the mountains and tower above the hills. And all the nations shall stream to it. And the many peoples shall go and say: "Come, let us go up to the Mount of GOD, to the House of the God of Jacob—that He may instruct us in His ways, that we may walk in His paths." For from Zion shall come forth Torah, and the word of GOD from Jerusalem....[21]

Anyone who is interested in the Laws of *Bnei Noach* and Divine worship for non-Jews is probably familiar with all of the above. The introductory and technical aspects of the seven universal commandments have been treated in the past in other books, some of which were written by Jewish authorities in Torah.

Revealing the Mystical

In this book we intend to introduce a completely novel aspect of the Laws of *Bnei Noach*. If the *Bnei Noach* commitment to the One God is to take root and flourish it must turn into a spirited and creative form of religious experience and expression. The key for achieving this lies in the mystical dimension of the Torah. By presenting the mystical aspects of the Laws of *Bnei Noach*, as derived from Kabbalah and Chassidut, the traditions of Jewish mysticism that reveal the inner dimension of the teachings of the Torah, this book will offer the reader the more spiritual and philosophical-theoretical aspects of the Divine service of righteous gentiles, while at the same time, opening up new avenues for religious expression. With this task in mind, we turn to the principles of faith entailed in the Laws of *Bnei Noach*.

Notes:

1. Based on Exodus 34:28 and Deuteronomy 4:13.
2. Rav Sa'adiah Ga'on, the 10th century religious leader of the Jewish people, wrote an entire volume in verse form on this topic by the name of the *Azharot* (see also *Rashi* to Exodus 24:14). In later generations, the commentary *Heichal Habrachah* written by the 18th century Komarna Rebbe, Rabbi Yitzchak Yehudah Yechiel Safrin, stands out in this genre.

   That the Torah contains 613 commandments (for Jews) was passed down from the Talmudic sages; see *Makot* 23b and 24a.
3. Most notably in the introduction to *Sefer Hachinuch*.
4. Genesis 6:9 thru 11:32.
5. Ibid. 6:10.
6. Of Abraham, the first Jew, the Torah says that God commanded him: "Walk before me and be earnest," (Ibid. 17:1) indicating that the Torah expects the Jewish people to be able to "walk before," that is, to lead God. At the same time the ideal type of religious experience for a non-Jew is to flow, i.e., to follow, or walk with the Divine.
7. Ibid. 6:11-13.
8 Ibid. chapter 9.
9. Ibid. 9:3-5.
10. The sages are of one opinion that six commandments, excluding the prohibition of eating a limb from a live animal, had already been given to Adam. Regarding the prohibition regarding a limb,

there are two opinions: according to one, this prohibition was also given to Adam. According to another opinion, Noah was the first to receive this instruction. See also p. 78.

11. *Sanhedrin* 46a; Maimonides, *Hilchot Melachim*, chapters 9 and 10.

12. See *Zohar* III, 73a.

13. Actually, God made two separate covenants with Abraham, the first over the Land of Israel (Genesis 15:18) and the second over circumcision (Ibid. 9), both with the common objective of choosing a people to inherit the chosen land.

14. The Torah states that "through Isaac your descendants shall be named" (Genesis 21:12). The sages explain that "through Isaac" limits which of Isaac's offspring will indeed be called the descendants of Abraham, specifically, referring to Jacob (and his children) alone (*Nedarim* 31a).

15. Genesis 32:29.

16. Exodus chapter 20, and elsewhere.

17. *Makot* 24a.

18. Some of these verses are:

"Thus said GOD: 'Israel is My son, My firstborn'" (Exodus 4:22).

"Now therefore, if you will obey My voice and keep My covenant, then you shall be My own treasure among all peoples; for all the earth is Mine; And you shall be to Me a kingdom of priests, and a holy nation" (Exodus 19:5-6).

"And I will dwell among the children of Israel, and will be their God. And they shall know that I am GOD their God, that brought them out of the land of Egypt that I may dwell among them; I am GOD their God" (Exodus 29:45-46).

"For you are a holy people to GOD your God; GOD your God has chosen you to be a special people to Himself, above all peoples that are upon the face of the earth. GOD did not set his love upon you, nor did He choose you because you were more in number than any people; for you were the fewest of all peoples; but because GOD loved you..." (Deuteronomy 7:6-8).

"You are the children of GOD your God.... For you are a holy people to GOD your God, and GOD has chosen you to be a special people to Himself, above all the nations that are upon the earth" (Deuteronomy 14:1-2).

19. Exodus 19:5-6.

20. Isaiah 49:6.

21. Ibid. 2:3.

Principles of Faith

1

As stressed in traditional Jewish writings, the core of all religious practice and the principle underlying all Divine worship is faith. As explained in Kabbalah, faith is the highest power of the soul, lying well beyond the reach of the rational mind, floating, as it were, above comprehension.

Although the most fundamental of the *Bnei Noach* commandments is the prohibition of the worship of other gods, the question must still be raised whether *Bnei Noach* are actually required to *believe* in God? This may seem like a strange question to ask, for why would anyone be committed to perform God's commandments if he or she does not believe in Him? However, it may seem less puzzling if we consider that there are many situations in life when a person loses conscious faith in the Almighty, yet continues to follow the Torah's commandments, forgoing questions of faith to a later time.

Furthermore, it is common to find people that perform religious commandments for a variety of reasons other than their belief in God. It may be that they do so because of tradition (as children they were raised with these practices), because of collective cultural values (their society prescribes it), or even just to alleviate social pressure (their peers would not associate with them if they did not), all without believing that God exists or that He commanded them to perform these acts.

At the present, there are relatively few *Bnei Noach* in the world so these external reasons for performing the *Bnei Noach* commandments may not seem to be very prominent in anyone's life. But, as the numbers increase, as the prophets foresaw, and people become second and third generation *Bnei Noach* living in large communities or even cultures that practice these commandments, the question of obligatory faith will become more and more important.

The Thirteen Principles of Jewish Faith

Indeed, talking of faith in God is quite vague. What exactly does faith in God include? What are the articles or principles of faith as delineated by the Torah? And, are they different for Jews and for non-Jews?

Though faith is a super-rational faculty, and therefore not normally subject to translation into a limited set of logical ordered principles, about 850 years ago, Maimonides — arguably the greatest authority on Jewish law and Torah thought[1] — compiled a list of 13 principles of Jewish faith.[2] They are:

1. God is the Creator and is responsible for all that happens.
2. God is One
3. God is not corporeal.
4. God is non-temporal.
5. God alone should be worshiped.
6. Prophecy is true.
7. The prophecy of Moses is primary and true.
8. The Torah is complete

9. The Torah is eternal.
10. There is Divine Providence.
11. God gives reward and punishment
12. The Messiah will arrive
13. God will resurrect the dead

As argued by later authorities,[3] Maimonides 13 principles all stem from 3 more general principles:

1. Faith in the Oneness and Singularity of the Almighty, out of which stem the first through the fifth principles;
2. Faith in the Torah's universal and everlasting verity as the expression of God's Will, out of which stem the sixth through the ninth principles; and,
3. Faith in reward and punishment based on each individual's conduct, from which stem the tenth through the thirteenth principles.

Of course, these three principles themselves are all an elaboration of the Torah's all inclusive expression of faith in the absolute Oneness of God: "Hear O' Israel, GOD is our God, GOD is One."[4]

Covenant Numbers

So, we now have that the most general principle of faith in the absolute Oneness of God divides into three more specific principles, which in turn divide into the thirteen principles listed by Maimonides. This numerical progression from 1 to 3 to 13 is part of a mystical series of numbers that is based in the Torah's oral tradition regarding the word "covenant" as it appears in the Written Torah. For this reason the numbers in this mystical series are known as "covenant numbers."

The traditional source for the series of covenant numbers is found in a Mishnah that states: "Circumcision is great, for thirteen covenants were made on it."[5] As explained by the Talmudic commentaries this statement refers to 13 instances of the word "covenant" (in its different grammatical forms) found in the verses that describe how God commanded Abraham to perform circumcision.[6] That circumcision in this Mishnah is described as "great" is not only qualitative but also quantitative. Hence, the Mishnah, as explained by the commentaries, is noting that the word "covenant" appears in these verses more times than it does in reference to other covenants chronicled in the Torah. Specifically, the commentaries explain that the Mishnah is comparing the thirteen times that the word "covenant" appears in reference to circumcision, the covenant made between God and Abraham, to the three times that it appears in reference to the covenant made between God and the Jewish people with the giving of the Torah.[7] It is also comparing the thirteen "covenants" of circumcision to the single "covenant" appearing in the verses describing how God promised the Land of Canaan to Abraham.[8] We now know the source of the three numbers, 1, 3, and 13, in this series.

But as mentioned above, before making the covenants with Abraham (regarding the Land of Canaan and circumcision) and with the Jewish people (regarding the Torah), the Almighty made a covenant with Noah. God promised that he would not destroy the world again by flood. In the verses in the Torah describing this covenant, the word "covenant" (in its various grammatical forms) appears seven times. Thus the complete series begins with the numbers 1, 3, 7, and 13.[9] Without getting too far ahead of ourselves, let us hint that the 7 instances of the word "covenant" found in the verses describing God's covenant with Noah correspond to the 7 *Bnei Noach* commandments (and to the 7 colors of the rainbow, the sign of the covenant between God and Noah), as will be explained more fully later on.

The Seven Principles of Faith for *Bnei Noach*

The series of covenant numbers thus begins with the numbers: 1, 3, 7, 13.[10] How fitting it is then that *Bnei Noach* should possess 7 principles of faith. Indeed, looking at Maimonides 13 Principles of Faith, we can see that before dividing into three general categories they first clearly divide into 7 more specific categories, as follows:

1. Faith in the existence of God the Creator
2. Faith in the Oneness of God
3. We should worship only God
4. The verity of prophecy
5. The eternal truth of the Torah
6. Reward and punishment
7. The ultimately good destiny of creation

These 7 principles of faith, which cover the basic tenets of faith for *Bnei Noach*, beautifully correspond to the seven Laws of *Bnei Noach*, and as such can be seen as their inner essence and spirit. Whereas six of these seven laws are usually stated negatively, i.e., as prohibitions, these articles of faith are positive in nature. Therefore, teaching each commandment with its corresponding principle provides a more balanced view on the *Bnei Noach* faith and commitment:

Faith in the existence of God the Creator clearly gives positive expression to the prohibition against blasphemy.

Faith in the Oneness of God is obviously the positive expression of the prohibition against idolatry.

While the second principle excludes worshiping any other being as a deity, the third principle (that man was created to worship God alone) deals with our obligation to worship the Almighty. In the Talmud,[11] not recognizing that God is the origin of all blessing, not thanking Him for the good things we possess in life, is likened to stealing from one's parents. Knowing that God is the source of all good, we turn to Him, and only to Him, in worship and prayer. Worship is thus seen to begin with not stealing from God that which He rightly deserves—the conscious awareness that all that we have, even our very existence, derives from Him. Thus this principle is the positive aspect of the prohibition against thievery, and as such, it implies that *Bnei Noach* should indeed have a book of prayers and make blessings over food,[12] etc., as will be discussed further in chapter 5.

The fourth principle of faith in the truth of prophecy acknowledges that man was created in the image of God, and is therefore able to commune with God in prophecy.[13] Hence, this principle reflects the basic sanctity of human life and thus it represents the positive aspect of the prohibition against murder.

The Talmud explains that sexual cravings are the most powerful force dissuading people from following the Torah. They are the "spirit of folly"[14] that induce one to bypass the injunctions of the Torah, creating the illusion that the violation of these prohibitions will not sever our conscious connection with the Almighty. Thus, the fifth principle, professing faith in the eternal nature of the Torah—whose directives comprise the way of life and are the basis of our connection with the Creator—provides the positive application of the prohibition against adultery. Following this principle, throughout the book of Proverbs the Torah is likened to a woman of valor to whom her husband forever remains loyal.

The sixth principle, the belief in God's reward and punishment based on His Providence over our actions, corresponds to the injunction to establish courts of law. Just courts of law are indeed a human expression of Divine Providence and justice.

To date, the image of Noah's dove and the rainbow, the sign of God's covenant with him, serve as the universal symbols for the peace and brotherhood that we all yearn for. According to Maimonides,[15] the one commandment that was given to Noah, in addition to the six that had previously been given to Adam, is the prohibition against eating a limb from a living animal. The final article of faith in the ultimately good destiny awaiting mankind is the mystical stipulation of this commandment for *Bnei Noach*. Though the commandment does not prohibit the consumption of animals entirely, it does preclude treating them with cruelty and causing them pain, thus foreshadowing a positive ecological vision of mankind as it will be in a more rectified future. In the Bible, the salvation of man is tied directly with the salvation of animals: "Man and animal shall You save, O' God."[16] The prohibition against eating the flesh of a living animal thus encourages our faith in the rectified and good future awaiting all of creation, as one.

Faith and Prayer

Every Jewish male above the age of thirteen is legally obligated to pray three times a day. Do *Bnei Noach* have anything of a similar obligation?

As we shall see in chapter 6, the House of God is described in the Bible as a house of prayer for all people, indicating that the Almighty yearns that all people come to pray before Him. There is a special category in Jewish law for non-obligatory devotion to the Almighty that merits reward, it is called "one who acts without being commanded."[17] Thus, a non-Jew, who takes it upon him or herself to pray to God merits reward.

In an attempt to answer this question from a halachic perspective, Rabbi Moshe Feinstein, one of the most important authorities in Jewish law in the previous generation, wrote a *teshuvah*, a halachic response, analyzing the question of prayer for non-Jews in depth. In his reply, Rabbi Feinstein argued that since the first individuals to establish rites of prayer were Abraham, Isaac, and Jacob (each of whom established one of the three daily prayers), therefore non-Jews, who by definition are not descended from the three Jewish patriarchs, are not obligated to pray on a regular, daily basis.

However, because the non-Jew is free from the obligation of daily prayers does not mean that he or she may not or should not pray. On the contrary, a non-Jew may turn to God in prayer at all times (as, of course, is the same for a Jew). In particular, Rabbi Feinstein rules that if a non-Jew is in trouble, or in pain, and beseeches the Almighty to help, then prayer takes on a completely different meaning. In such a case, prayer gives voice to one's faith in the Almighty as the Ruler of the universe, as the One to whom it is fitting to turn to in times of trouble for aid and in times of joy for thanksgiving. Such faith, though not explicitly mentioned as one of the seven Laws of *Bnei Noach*, is nonetheless implied,[18] and indeed is the foundation upon which all of the *Bnei Noach* commandments rest. In other words, without conscious faith in God—faith so real that one is motivated to turn to God in prayer in times of need—it is impossible to perform the *Bnei Noach* commandments.

Notes:

1. Maimonides is the Greek form of Rabbi Moshe ben Maimon, also known by his acronym, the Rambam (1135-1204).

2. Though Maimonides was evidently not aware of it, in the *Zohar* it is written that faith is indeed based on thirteen principles (*Zohar* III, 62b), which correspond to the 13 *tikunei dikna* (garments of the beard)—the 13 principles of Divine effluence that run from the *sefirah* of crown (super-consciousness) to the conscious *sefirot* and that are symbolically associated with the parts of the human beard. From this correspondence of the 13 principles of faith with the 13 *tikunei dikna* we learn that principles of faith, like the *sefirah* of crown itself, exhibit a paradoxical quality. On the one hand they are verily super-rational, but on the other they are well-defined and ordered.

   The paradoxical nature of the 13 Principles of Faith can be illustrated numerically: 13 · 102 (the numerical value of the word "faith," in Hebrew, אֱמוּנָה) = 1326. 1326 is the numerical value of the third verse of the Priestly Blessing: "May God lift His countenance upon you and give you peace" (יִשָּׂא יֱ־הוה פָּנָיו אֵלֶיךָ וְיָשֵׂם לְךָ שָׁלוֹם). The first word of this verse יִשָּׂא stems from the same root as the Hebrew term for "paradox" (נְשִׂיאַת הַפָּכִים).

3. Rabbi Joseph Albo, *Sefer Ha'ikarim*, part A, chapter 4.

4. Deuteronomy 6:4.

5. *Nedarim* 31b.

6. Genesis chapter 17.

7. *Berachot* 48b and commentaries there.

8. Genesis 15:18.

9. Chronologically, the order of the covenants is the covenant made with Noah (7), followed by the covenant with Abraham regarding the Land of Israel (1), followed by the covenant with

Abraham regarding circumcision (13), and finally the covenant with the Jewish people regarding the Torah (3). But, mathematically, the order of the numbers in the series is of course 1, 3, 7, and 13.

10. The mathematical expression of this series is: for all integers n, $f[n] = n^2 \perp n \perp 1$.

11. *Berachot* 35b.

12. This connection between thievery and worship was first made by the *Torah Temimah*, who argued that it implies that non-Jews should bless God before eating or taking pleasure form something in the world.

13. "God said: Let us create man in our image and after our likeness" (Genesis 1:26).

14. *Sotah* 3a.

15. Maimonides, *Hilchot Melachim* 9:1.

16. Psalms 36:7.

17. *Avodah Zarah* 3a.

18. With regard to Jews there are two opinions whether faith in God is counted as one of the 613 commandments. Maimonides and others write that faith is indeed a commandment, while others, like the *Bahag* (*Ba'al Halachot Gedolot*, an early codex of Torah law), write that faith is a prerequisite to all 613 commandments and therefore cannot be counted as one of them. Clearly, the non-Jew who is not explicitly commanded to believe in God still requires faith as a prerequisite to the seven Laws of *Bnei Noach*.

    The essential point of disagreement between these two opinions is explained in length in *Derech Mitzvotecha* (44d ff.) by the third Lubavitcher Rebbe. There he explains that when faith is treated as a commandment in its own right it motivates meditative prayer; when treated as a prerequisite, it motivates prayer from the heart in times of need. Thus, for the non-Jew, though meditative prayer is not a commandment, prayer in times of need certainly is.

Monotheism

The Apparent Plurality of the One God

Many false beliefs have been propagated throughout the world. Therefore, it is important that at the outset of this book, we clarify some basic Torah truths which are often presented by other religions in a distorted manner, sometimes in a deliberate attempt to deceive.

First of all, God is absolutely One. God, the Creator, possesses no intrinsic duality or plurality, in any form whatsoever. All the apparent plurality that people see in the One God is a result of the process of creation and our inability to exist in the infinite Presence of the Almighty.

To understand the relationship between God's absolute Oneness and the multi-faceted manifestations by which He is revealed in our world, we turn to the Kabbalistic description of creation. Kabbalah teaches that in the most general terms creation consists of two stages, both described using the same Hebrew word: *tzimtzum*. In Hebrew, *tzimtzum* means either "to diminish" or "to concentrate." God began the creative process by diminishing (the first meaning of *tzimtzum*) His infinite light in order to make space, as it were, for His creation.

The final limit of any diminishing process is a reduction to zero, or total disappearance. This is what is implied in

Kabbalah by the term *tzimtzum* in relation to God's initial contraction of His infinite light in order to create room for worlds to exist. Worlds describe a state of being seemingly outside of God.[1] The first *tzimtzum* (as diminishing) allowed God to seemingly disappear entirely from the stage upon which the second stage of creation would play out.

The second stage of the creative process also consists of a *tzimtzum*, but this time in the sense of a concentration. Kabbalah describes that God projected a ray of His previously concealed infinite light (referred to as the *kav*) back into the seeming void created by the initial *tzimtzum*. God's infinite light, i.e., His infinite revelation, was concentrated into a thin finite ray. Worlds were then created around this ray of light.[2] The ray of infinite light is to the cosmos like the soul is to the body.[3] The ray of infinite light is the sustaining and animating force within, but, like the soul in the human body, its presence remains concealed.[4]

God's infinite light, were we able to experience it directly, would reveal His absolute singularity and Oneness. But, because of the *tzimtzum*, in our normal state of consciousness, we are only able to experience the revelation of God's nature through its plurality of manifestations. Nonetheless, one of the most basic tenets of Jewish faith is that the diminishing and disappearance of the infinite light should not be understood literally; i.e., they were not "events" that transformed God's nature as the Creator. Rather, the disappearance of God's infinite light from the place He prepared for created reality is only from our perspective. From God's perspective—"I GOD have not changed."[5] The original infinite light remains within the apparent void and continues to shine (from God's perspective) just as it did before the creative process and the

initial *tzimtzum*. Only from our eyes has the light disappeared.
And so with regard to the ray of light (the *kav*), from God's
perspective, the sense of infinite expanse remains within the
apparent thin ray of light that permeates primordial space,
even though we remain oblivious to it. In our world, which is
the last of the worlds created around the ray of infinite light
and which is physical and finite, God appears to us in many
manifestations.[6] But God is, was, and always shall be One and
only One.[7]

God is One, Singular, and Unique

In referring to God's essence, the sages describe Him as "One,
Singular, and Unique."[8]

One implies that God's very essence permeates all of reality.

Singular, which can also be translated as "only One,"
implies that His existence is the only true existence. To quote
Maimonides, "All other existence is dependent upon His
existence."[9]

In Kabbalah and Chassidut we are taught that *unique*, in
relation to God, means that He defies logic. He is "the paradox
of paradoxes."[10] He absolutely transcends any polarity or
opposites. In the context of creation, nature and the
supernatural miracle are one from His perspective.

According to the sages, that God is unique is revealed
through His essential Name, known as the Tetragrammaton
(because it is made up of four letters). Because we are
forbidden to pronounce this Name as it is written, we refer to
it by rearranging its letters to spell the word *Havayah*, which
literally means "Being." The sages refer to the
Tetragrammaton as the "unique Name" (in contrast to other
Names of God that appear in the Bible[11]).

The Divine consciousness within every Jewish soul is in effect a spiritual legacy that Jews have inherited from the three patriarchs: Abraham, Isaac, and Jacob. In particular, faith in God as "One" is Abraham's spiritual legacy (whom God called "one"[12]) ; faith in God as "Singular" comes from Isaac (who is called "single one"[13]); and, faith in God as the absolutely "Unique [One]" is inherited from Jacob (who is referred to in Rabbinic literature as the "choice [i.e., unique] among the fathers"[14]).

Since God's infinity is incomprehensible to our finite minds, we can only relate to God through His manifestations and as mentioned, they usually exhibit plurality. Let us give a few examples to illustrate this point.

Transcendence vs. Immanence

Our first example is God's dual manifestation as both transcendent and immanent. By virtue of this particular manifestation we are able to relate to God as being simultaneously both beyond our world and the mundane reality of our lives (His transcendence),[15] yet paradoxically, also within our world and every facet and experience of our personal lives (His immanence).

Let us say a few more words about the deeper meaning of God's transcendence vs. His immanence. In Kabbalah and Chassidut, God's transcendence and immanence are referred to as "the light surrounding all worlds" and "the light filling all worlds," respectively. They also correspond to the revelation of God's infinite light before the initial *tzimtzum* and to the light of the *kav*, as described above.

In Hebrew, the numerical value of the word for "surrounding" (סוֹבֵב) is 70, the same as that for the word "secret" (סוֹד). The numerical value of the word for "filling" (מְמַלֵּא) is 111, the same as that for the word "wonder" (פֶּלֶא). This alludes to the fact that God's transcendent nature is the *secret* around but not consciously within every point of reality, while His immanence, His revealed presence within each and every one of us, is the *wonder* of reality.

The sum of the numerical values of the two phrases "surrounding all worlds" (סוֹבֵב כָּל עָלְמִין) and "filling all worlds" (מְמַלֵּא כָּל עָלְמִין) is 681, which is also the sum of the numerical values of the two words "heavens" (שָׁמַיִם) and "earth" (אֶרֶץ). This teaches us that our experience of God's transcendence is similar to experiencing the heavens above and surrounding us, while our experience of God's immanence is similar to experiencing the earth upon which we walk, the foundation (or grounding principle) of our conscious lives.

And so we may conclude that the very first verse of the Torah, "In the beginning God created the heavens and the earth," alludes to the most fundamental dual manifestation of God, the Creator, in our lives—His manifestation as "surrounding all worlds," "the heavens," and His manifestation as "filling all worlds," "the earth." Indeed, the very first letter of the Torah is a *beit* (ב) whose numerical value is 2, alluding to the dualities that are inherent to the natural world beginning with the most basic duality of the heavens and the earth, which originates from the Creator's dual manifestation of transcendence and immanence.[16]

The Four Letters

Another multiple manifestation of God is revealed through the four letters of His essential Name, *Havayah*, just mentioned.

The literal meaning of God's essential Name is: "continuously bringing reality into existence." But even within this seemingly simple reference of God as Creator, each of His essential Name's four letters (*yud, hei, vav, hei*) refers to one of the four stages of the ongoing creative process: contraction, expansion, extension, expansion.[17]

In addition to its literal meaning, God's essential Name, *Havayah*, is understood to be an acronym for "[He] was, is, and will be."[18] Within time, God is eternal. Moreover, He is above time. Time itself is a creation and does not exist in God's infinite light before the creative process. God's eternal nature manifests in creation in three different ways, each comprising itself four levels that correspond to the four letters of His essential Name. They are His: omnipresence, omnipotence, and omniscience (also called Divine Providence).

Likewise, God appears in even more complex manifestations, comprising five, six, seven, or more facets. Judaism, and especially its mystical teachings are replete with multi-faceted models that describe God's manifestation in our reality. Most famous among these are the ten *sefirot*—the Divine emanations of creation, the thirteen attributes of Divine mercy,[19] and the twenty-two letters of the Hebrew alphabet.[20] Nonetheless, all of these—when traced back to their ultimate source in God's infinite light before its contraction—return to a state of absolute Oneness.

All Numbers Return to One

The true monotheist feels that everything, even that which seems to have a dual nature, is in the end unified in God. Nothing more than numbers reflects the diversification of reality. After all, 2 is definitely more multitudinous than 1, and

3 even more so than 2, and so on. Therefore, the question arises of whether monotheism treats numbers in any special manner.

The Torah commands the Jewish people to relate the story of the Exodus on the first night of Passover.[21] At the end of the traditional retelling of the exodus, it is customary to recite (or sing) a poem titled "Who knows 'one'?" The poem develops through a series of questions and answers regarding the symbolism of each of the numbers from one to thirteen. The first question is: "Who knows 'one'," meaning, who knows what one symbolizes. The answer that follows is:

> "I know 'one!' 'One' is our God in heaven and on earth."

This statement, that God is One in the heavens and the earth then serves as the refrain for all the other stanzas of the poem.

> "Who knows 'two'?" is answered by "I know 'two!' 'Two' are the tablets of the covenant."

But then the refrain is added: 'One' is our God in heaven and on earth."

> "Who knows 'three'?" is answered by "I know 'three'! Three are the forefathers. Two are the tablets of the covenant," and then the refrain: "One is our God in heaven and on earth."

In the final stanza we have the following:

> Who knows "thirteen?" I know "thirteen." "Thirteen" are the Divine attributes of mercy. "Twelve" are the tribes of Israel. "Eleven" are the stars [of Joseph's dream]. "Ten" are the Ten Commandments. "Nine" are the months of pregnancy. "Eight" are the days of circumcision.

> "Seven" are the days of the week. "Six" are the
> orders of the Mishnah. "Five" are the books of the
> Torah. "Four" are the mothers. "Three" are the
> fathers. "Two" are the tablets of the covenant.
> "One" is our God in heaven and on earth.

Every number (not only those from 1 to 13) possesses an
intrinsic spiritual meaning, a part of the collective
consciousness of the Jewish people and of all people whose
souls and psyches are linked to the Torah. Each number
manifests a particular Torah "set" of Divine manifestations
including what may at first appear as a mundane natural
phenomenon, such as the nine months of pregnancy. But, most
importantly for the monotheist, after every answer regarding
the number at hand, we "return" through all of the previous
numbers until we reach the number one: "One is our God in
heaven and on earth." All returns to One, for the One God is
the origin of all the plurality in our world.

God, Torah, and Israel

In the *Zohar*, the classic text of Kabbalah, as well as in other
Jewish sources,[22] we find that there are three manifestations of
Godliness, which are considered essentially One. These are
God,[23] the Torah, and Israel (meaning, the Jewish people).[24]

As explained above, there is nothing special that
distinguishes the number three from any other number, for the
complex manifestations of the Almighty appear in conjunction
with all numbers. After the initial contraction of His infinite
light, God—the absolute One—can and does appear to finite
consciousness in any number of manifestations that He so
desires.

Without the blemishes and misconceptions introduced by the limits imposed on us by finite consciousness (which is also the origin of all sin) the transcendent unity behind these multiple manifestations can be truly appreciated. The state of being that is unhindered by our finite consciousness and which can perceive the Divine as the absolute One, is known in Kabbalah as the World of Emanation (*Olam Ha'atzilut*), the highest of the four general states of reality described as "worlds."[25]

Minds originating in the three lower worlds of Creation, Formation, and Action (whose state of consciousness has fallen from that of Emanation) tend to separate, differentiate, and divide, and thereby perceive reality as pluralistic. This tendency may easily degenerate into idol worship.

Monotheistic consciousness, which started with Abraham, and which became the spiritual inheritance of all Jews, originates in the World of Emanation, where nothing stands apart and separate from the Almighty. Because of this, monotheistic consciousness allows a person to see through the multiple manifestations of the Divine that seem to fill the world around us and thereby help him or her retain perfect faith in God's absolute Oneness. However, non-Jews did not receive Abraham's spiritual inheritance and therefore do not possess an innate monotheistic perspective on reality. Consequently, a non-Jew may believe, theoretically, that God is One. But, as soon as questions about God's actual manifestation in reality arise, in the mind of the non-Jew, the description of God tends to take on some form of plurality, the exact nature of which is irrelevant—it could be a duality, like the Chinese Yin and Yang, or a trinity, like the Christian model, all the way to full-fledged polytheism. The mind rooted in the consciousness of the three lower worlds[26] creates a division in God's true unity, a division that tends to degenerate into idol worship, as stated above.

The only remedy for this innate tendency to perceive God as a plurality (i.e., polytheism, or pantheism as the case may be) is for a non-Jew to bind his or her consciousness to the Torah's universal teachings. The essence of the Torah that lies within its every word is that God is absolutely One. That is the origin of the sages' saying that every word of the Torah is a Name of the Almighty.[27] The subliminal and conscious message forever transmitted by the Torah to both the Jew and the non-Jew is the message of God's absolute and undividable unity.

Returning to the threesome, of God, Torah, and Israel: the Torah is the wisdom and spirit of the Almighty, of which it is said: "He and His wisdom are one."[28] Israel is considered the Almighty's son, of whom it is said: "Israel is My son, My firstborn,"[29] and as such the Jewish nation represents an essence of the Father.

That said, it is essential to stress that no Jew would ever dream of regarding the people of Israel as an entity unto itself, and praying to it, God forbid! Such a thought does not even enter into Jewish consciousness (the consciousness of the World of Emanation, as explained above). The same is true with regard to the Torah. The Torah is the holy spirit of God. But no Jew would ever dream of relating to the Torah as an independent entity.[30] The monotheistic soul never makes the mistake of attaching independent reality to one of God's manifestations.

In this spirit, one should read the verses describing the Torah:

"GOD possessed me at the beginning of His way...
When He prepared the heavens, I was there...
When He marked out the foundations of the
earth... then I was beside Him... and my delight
[was] with the sons of men."[31]

The Torah is, as it were, the speaker of these verses. As
explained above, when relating to any number of
manifestations following the initial contraction of God's
infinite light, we must bear in mind that both before and after
the contraction, these manifestations remain absolutely One.
The paradox implicit in the Torah saying "I was beside God"
or "I was the tool of God in Creation" remains just that—a
paradox. The ultimate, absolute root of the souls of Israel, the
son of God, also existed before the initial contraction,
absolutely One with God.

This paradox is one that a consciousness severed from
Emanation cannot appreciate. The only One to whom we pray
is God Himself. This is one of the Thirteen Principles of Faith
as discussed in the introduction.[32] True monotheistic
consciousness, even as it manifests after the initial contraction
(in the World of Emanation), is always connected to the
essence of God as was revealed in His infinite light before the
initial contraction that brought the plurality of His
manifestations into being.

We are further taught in the *Zohar* that the Torah serves as a
link between the created consciousness of Israel and the
infinite light of God. As a connecting intermediary, the Torah
is in its essence no more than the manifestation of God's
affinity to Israel and Israel's affinity to God. And so, the initial
three—God, the Torah, and Israel—can be seen to reduce to
two: God and Israel.[33] These three can also expand into four

(and thus correspond to the four letters of God's essential Name, as described above). In such a case, the single manifestation of the nation of Israel divides into the *tzadik* (the righteous Messianic figure present in every generation[34]) and the Jewish People (the Congregation of Israel, called *Kneset Yisrael*, in Hebrew). These two are then referred to as the Almighty's "son" and "daughter," respectively.[35]

The Mistaken Origin of the Trinity

However, as explained above, non-Jewish, non-monotheistic consciousness, is rooted in plurality, as will be explained presently. This is why, from the non-Jewish perspective, the "father," "son," and "the spirit of wisdom" appear as three separate entities. The claim of some that the trinity is meant to be perceived as one is immaterial, because the non-Jewish consciousness is unable to truly unify the three and to understand that their essence is one.

Instead, non-Jews perceive each of the three as possessing such a strong personality of its own that each is seen as existing independently.[36] The non-Jewish attempt to parody this ultimate secret of "three which are one" totally destroys the authenticity of the paradox of the concept.

Indeed, the belief in a trinity is nothing short of idolatry as defined by the Torah.[37]

Idolatry in any form is completely forbidden by God for all peoples. The prohibition against idolatry is the most fundamental of the seven Laws of *Bnei Noach*, and thus it is essential that the Torah's universal wisdom be taught to all people so that they too may perceive the true unity of God.

Misreading the Bible

In their attempt to persuade others (especially religiously uneducated Jews) to accept their beliefs, non-Jewish missionaries often misquote or misinterpret traditional Jewish sources. Let us examine one such distorted interpretation of the Biblical text, thereby unveiling the shallowness of the deception, and giving those contending with missionaries (whether Jews or righteous gentiles) a deeper understanding of the Torah's truths.

One particular passage from Isaiah is often the subject of such a deception by trinitarians. Unlike the text of the Torah, i.e., the Five Books of Moses, the text of the rest of the Bible (the Prophets and the Writings) cannot always be interpreted literally. As explained in the Talmud and elaborated on by Maimonides in length, Moses' prophecy differs from that of all other prophets. As God Himself bears witness to the uniqueness of Moses prophecy: "With him [Moses] I speak face to face, clearly and not in riddles."[38] Therefore, the text of the Five Books of Moses always has a straight-forward, literal interpretation (together with deeper, non-literal strata of meaning). But the prophecies of the other prophets recorded in the Bible often demand exclusively non-literal interpretation. To correctly understand their meaning, one must turn to the traditional translation to Aramaic, known as *Targum Yonatan*, and to the traditional commentaries of *Rashi*, Ibn Ezra, and *Radak*.

As explained above, the consciousness of the World of Emanation, the monotheistic consciousness that the authors of all of these traditional Jewish sources share, sees through what might to others seem like a plurality of sorts. They are therefore able to interpret the prophecy in the way similar to the manner in which Isaiah himself, who also shared the monotheistic consciousness, understood it.

In chapter 48 of Isaiah we find the following verses:

> (12) Listen to Me, O' Jacob, and Israel whom I have called; I am He, I am the First, I am also the Last. (13) My hand has also laid the foundation of the earth, and My right hand has spanned the heavens; When I call them, they stand up together. (14) All of you: assemble yourselves and hear, which among them has declared these things? He whom GOD loves, he will do His pleasure on Babylon, and his arm shall be on the Kasdim. (15) I have spoken, I have even called him; I have brought him, and he shall succeed in his way. (16) Come near to Me, hear this: I have not spoken in secret from the beginning, from the time that it was, there have I been; And now the Lord GOD has sent me and His spirit.[39]

The above verses form a self-contained portion of Isaiah's prophecy. Therefore, in the Masoretic text (the traditional Jewish Bible), they appear as a separate unit (*parashah*).[40]

Let us analyze the last verse of this portion, the source for the mistaken interpretation. Contrary to the Christian interpretation, this verse does not speak of three divine entities.

> Come near to Me, hear this: I have not spoken in secret from the beginning, from the time that it was, there have I been; And now the Lord God has sent me and His spirit.

The confusion lies in identifying who is saying which part of this verse, God or His prophet, Isaiah.

The *Targum* (also quoted in the beginning of *Rashi's* commentary) explains that God's final words are: "There have I been." According to the *Targum*, the remainder of the verse is spoken by Isaiah.

Rashi offers two additional possibilities for reading the verse. Either God concludes with the words "from the beginning," or it is Isaiah that speaks the entire verse, from beginning to end. According to the second possibility, *Rashi* explains that the prophet's soul was present when God made His decree (which the prophecy is addressing) even before his soul had descended to earth. From this we learn that Isaiah's soul, like every Jewish soul, was a part of God above before descending into a physical body. The explanation that the prophet's soul received its prophecy before descending into a human body is based on the *Midrash Tanchuma*, which attributes prophecy to the revelation of the Torah at Mt. Sinai. According to the *Midrash* just as all Jewish souls were present at the giving of the Torah (and all subsequent innovations in Torah originate in that event) so all the prophets received their prophecy at Mt. Sinai (regardless of when they actually delivered it). Ultimately, it will be revealed that each and every Jewish soul received a prophecy at Mt. Sinai, and all the people of God will be recognized as prophets.[41]

The *Radak* explains that a prophet sometimes hears the direct voice of God, and sometimes has a vision of an angel sent to speak with him. According to this, "His spirit" refers to the angel. The meaning of the verse is thus: "God has sent me, together with the angel who I saw in my prophecy, to speak with me and direct me."

Another reading of the word "His spirit" is "the spirit within me." The prophet thereby relates that he became inspired. This is the explanation of Rav Sa'adiah Gaon. The *vav* in the word *verucho* ("*and* His spirit") translates as "*with* His spirit." The meaning of the verse according to this reading is: "God has aroused His spirit within me, and with the power of that spirit has sent me to prophesize to the people."

In any case, although this verse does in fact relate to three: God, who decrees, the prophet who is God's messenger sent to declare His decree, and the angel sent to the prophet or the spirit of prophecy that dwells within the prophet, nonetheless, the rectified consciousness of the Jewish commentaries makes it clear that they do not represent three different divinities. Instead, either God has created a prophet and an angel or spirit of prophecy, or, the soul of the prophet and the spirit of prophecy were simply one with God before being created.

We conclude that the truly monotheistic consciousness inherent in the Jewish consciousness prevents incorrect readings of the Biblical text, where indeed such readings are plausible. We might say that the Jewish mind is hard-wired to seek the unity of God, while the still unrectified non-Jewish mind, void of a true monotheistic outlook, tends to find plurality where it does not exist.

Notes:

1. What appears to us as outside of God, to God is, as it were, inside Himself. In the words of the sages, "He is the place of the universe though the universe is not His place" (*Midrash Bereisheet Rabah* 68:9). This means that although in truth the universe and all of reality exists inside (i.e., as an indivisible part of) God, God does not, at present (until the coming of the Messiah) reveal His

absolute Presence within and throughout reality (including empty space).

2. Some of the original worlds were created and then destroyed, a calamity also known as the breaking of the vessels. The purpose of this destruction, on the spiritual plane, was the creation of the lowest of worlds, in which we live, a corporal reality containing both good and evil and granting us the ability to choose freely between the two antithetical poles.

3. In relation to the ray (the *kav*), the sages say that God (as explained above, the *kav* is indivisible from the essence of God's infinite light) is to the world as the soul is to the body (See *Berachot* 10a; *Midrash Vayikra Rabah*, 4; *Midrash Shocher Tov Tehillim*, 103).

4. To be more exact, in the Divine consciousness of the World of Emanation (*Atzilut*) the presence of the *kav*, the soul of creation, is revealed, whereas in the three lower worlds of Creation, Formation, and Action (*Beri'ah*, *Yetzirah*, and *Asiyah*), whose state of consciousness is separate from God, the presence of the *kav* is concealed.

5. Malachi 3:6.

6. For this reason we find that in the Bible, and even more so in Kabbalistic texts, God possesses many Names (and even more descriptive connotations, such as "the Merciful One"). Each Name (or connotation) designates a special manifestation of God in reality. Indeed, we are taught in Kabbalah that every word in the Torah conceals within itself a Name of God. Furthermore, the Messiah will reveal that the entire Torah, from beginning to end, is in essence one great Name of God. See *What You Need to Know About Kabbalah*, part III.

7. In Hebrew, "one" is *echad* (אֶחָד) and "single [one]" is *yachid* (יָחִיד).

8. In Hebrew, these three connotations of the Almighty—One, Singular, and Unique—are expressed as an idiom: אֶחָד יָחִיד וּמְיוּחָד. Treating the first letter, the *alef* (א), as equal to 1000 (a common practice in *gematria* as the letter's name—*alef*—can be read as *elef*,

which is the Hebrew word for "one thousand"), the numerical value of this idiom is exactly 1118, the same as the numerical value of the quintessential declaration of God's unity: "Hear O' Israel: GOD is our God, GOD is One" (שְׁמַע יִשְׂרָאֵל יְ־הוה אֱ־לֹהֵינוּ יְ־הוה אֶחָד). This idiom also contains exactly 13 letters; 13 is the numerical value of the word "one," אֶחָד.

9. Maimonides, *Hilchot Yesodei Hatorah* 1:1.

10. *Shut Harashba*, vol. 1, 418

11. See in length in part III of *What You Need to Know About Kabbalah*.

12. Isaiah 51:2.

13. Genesis 22:2, 12, and 16.

14. *Arizal's Sha'ar Hapsukim* to Genesis 27:25.

15. This is the secret of God's knowing all without interfering with our free choice. God's immanence is His Providence over all.

16. The sages explain that the first letter of the Torah, the *beit*, alludes to the Hebrew word for "blessing" (בְּרָכָה), which begins with a *beit*. The blessing in mind at the outset of creation is the Priestly Blessing (Numbers 6:24-26), which consists of three individual blessings. Three times the numerical value of the word for blessing (בְּרָכָה), 227, is 681, the same number that is the sum of the numerical values of "heavens" (שָׁמַיִם) and "earth" (אֶרֶץ)!

17. See *What You Need to Know About Kabbalah*, pp. 129-31.

18. In particular, the first letter of the Name *Havayah* (יְהוה), the *yud* (י), corresponds to "was" (before the beginning of creation), the third letter, the *vav* (ו), to "is" (throughout the six millenia of this world; ו = 6), and the common second and fourth letter, the *hei* (ה), to "will be." The reality of the future implied by "will be" manifests on two planes, as represented by the repetition of the letter *hei*. The second, or lower, *hei*, symbolizes the Messianic Era following the present order of this world, while the first, or higher *hei* symbolizes the revelation of God in the World to Come. Indeed, the consciousness of the end (the World to Come) is linked to the beginning (the essence of God's infinite light

before creation), and so the higher *hei* preceeds the *vav* of the present.

19. Exodus 34:6-7. See also *What You Need to Know About Kabbalah*, pp. 84-5.

20. Treated in length in *The Hebrew Letters: Channels of Creative Consciousness*.

21. "You shall tell your son on that day, saying, 'It is because of what GOD did for me when I came out of Egypt'" (Exodus 13:8).

22. Based on the *Zohar* (III, 73a), we often find in Chassidic texts the statement that, "Israel, the Torah and the Holy One Blessed Be He are One."

23. It is explained in Kabbalah that this particular manifestation of the Almighty refers to *partzuf ze'eir anpin*, one of the 12 major *partzufim*, i.e., direct manifestations of the Almighty in every world.

24. This statement in the *Zohar* gives a physical correspondence to the parallel statement that appears in Jewish philosophy: "He, His thought, and the object of His thought are all One." "He" of course corresponds to God Himself; "His thought" corresponds to the Torah; and, "the object of His thought" corresponds to Israel.

25. About the four worlds as states of consciousness, see in *What You Need to Know About Kabbalah*, pp. 133ff.

26. Since in fact there are three lower worlds, the number three reflects pluralistic consciousness, with the image of God as a parent deriving from the World of Creation, the image of God as spirit deriving from the World of Formation and the corporal image of God as a son deriving from the World of Action.

27. *Zohar* II, 87a.

28. Rabbi Moshe Cordovero, *Pardes Rimonim* 4:10.

29. Exodus 4:22. The numerical values of the three Hebrew words that comprise this phrase—"Israel is My son, My firstborn," בְּנִי בְכֹרִי יִשְׂרָאֵל—are 62, 232, and 541. They can be analyzed as

forming a segment of an ascending quadratic series, whose proceeding and following members are discovered by the process referred to as "finite differences," as follows:

31		62		232		541		989		1576		2302
	31		170		309		448		587		726	
	139		139		139		139		139		

The number that proceeds 62 in the series is its half, 31, the value of the Name of God by which He called Israel (Genesis 32:29), El (אֵ־ל). 31 is the lowest number, or base, of the infinite series (a quadratic series is graphically represented as a parabola). The three numbers following 541 are 989, 1576, and 2302. Together, the sum of the first seven numbers in the series ("all sevens are dear" – *Midrash Vayikra Rabah* 29:11) is 5733 = 13 · 441; 13 is the numerical value of "one," אֶחָד, and "love," אַהֲבָה, and 441 = 21², and is the numerical value of "truth" (אֱמֶת).

5733 is also 7 · 819, meaning that the average value of the first seven numbers in the series is 819. 819 is equal to the sum of all the squares from 1² to 13², also known as the pyramid of 13. It is also the numerical value of the connotation for God's Oneness, "simple unity" (אַחְדוּת פְּשׁוּטָה). Thus, "Israel is My son, My firstborn" alludes to the ultimate, absolute truth of God's simple unity that permeates the consciousness of Israel, which will be fully revealed in the "Days of the Messiah" (which in Hebrew also equals 819, יְמוֹת הַמָּשִׁיחַ). The sages teach that even today, before the arrival of the true Messiah, "David, the King of Israel, is alive and present" (a well known Hebrew idiom: דָּוִד מֶלֶךְ יִשְׂרָאֵל חַי וְקַיָם, whose numerical value is also 819) in every generation.

30. Following the statement that "the Holy One and the Torah are one" (see *Zohar* II, 90b).

31. Proverbs 8:22-31.

32. See pp. 22ff.

33. We saw above, that the two tablets of the covenant given to Moses at Mt. Sinai are the most primal example of a couple in Jewish consciousness. The first five of the Ten Commandments, which are engraved on the first tablet, all fall under the category of those commandments which regulate the relationship between man and God (honoring one's parents, the fifth commandment, is in fact an expression of honoring God, for God together with one's parents act together as "partners" in procreation, with God, who bestows the soul and human consciousness, as the principal "partner"), while the second five, engraved on the second tablet regulate the relationship between man and his fellow man. Thus, the two tablets themselves correspond to God and to Israel (after which we return to the basic consciousness of "One is our God in heaven and on earth").

34. Of whom God says: "You are My son" (Psalms 2:7).

35. Just as God calls the Messiah "My son," so He calls the people of Israel "My daughter" (*Midrash Shemot Rabah* 52:4). In Hebrew, the sum of the numerical values of "My son" (בְּנִי, 62) and "My daughter" (בְּתִּי, 412) is equal to the numerical value of the word for "knowledge" (דַעַת, 474), the *sefirah* that unites the "son" and the "daughter."

The understanding that Israel are both the son and daughter of the Almighty, gives us a full correspondence to the four letters of *Havayah*, which represent the ideal family of father (God), mother (the Torah), son (the Messianic figure present within every generation), daughter (the Congregation of Israel, *Keneset Yisrael*), as follows:

י	father	God
ה	mother	Torah
ו	son	Messianic figure
ה	daughter	Congregation of Israel

Every commandment is intended to manifest Godliness on earth and to reflect the secret of God's essential Name, *Havayah*. This is most beautifully apparent in the first commandment of the Torah, the commandment to be fruitful and multiply, which according to the sages (*Yevamot* 61b) means giving birth to at least one son and one daughter, thereby emulating God, the Creator, by making an ideal family, reflecting the secret of the Name *Havayah*.

The numerical value of all four parts of this correspondence in Hebrew, יְשְׂרָאֵל מָשִׁיחַ תּוֹרָה יהוה׳ is equal to 1536 = 4 · 384, meaning that the average value of each element is 384. But, 384 is the numerical value of the phrase "the Messiah of God" (מָשִׁיחַ ׳יהוה), the combined value of the words corresponding to the *yud* and the *vav* of the Name *Havayah*, indicating that the Messianic spirit permeates the ideal family.

36. As explained by modern researchers, the shattering of God's Oneness into separate figures each representing a particular character trait and treated as a separate deity is a product of the mythological mindset. In respect to Christianity, it is a product of the Greek and Roman mythological traditions, whose peoples adopted the newly invented religion.

37. Maimonides *Hilchot Ma'achalot Asurot* 11:7, *Hilchot Avodah Zarah* 9:4; *Ran* on *Avodah Zarah* 57a.

38. Numbers 12:8.

39. 48:12-16.

40. Altogether, the word "I" appears seven times in this *parashah*. The Hebrew word for "I" (אֲנִי) is a permutation of the word meaning "nothingness" (אַיִן). The word for "nothingness" alludes to the almost identical word meaning "eye" (עַיִן), where the first letter, *alef*, is replaced by the letter closest to it phonetically, the letter *ayin*. In Kabbalah it is explained that these two letters, *alef* and *ayin* form a spiritual pair, like a soul and a body, with the *alef*, the first letter of the alphabet forever enclothed within the letter *ayin*. Thus, the internal essence of the "eye" is the Divine

"nothingness." In English too, the words "I" and "eye" are phonetically the same.

In the Bible, we find that God has seven "eyes" (Zachariah 4:10). This is obviously not meant to be taken literally, but conveys the secret that in His Providence, God overlooks and judges creation from seven perspectives. Just as God possesses seven "eyes," He is revealed in these verses from the book of Isaiah to have seven "I"s.

41. Until that time, the prophecy that each Jew received serves to inspire his novel interpretations of the Torah, as explained in the *Tanya* (*Igeret Hakodesh* 26). This is further alluded to by the total number of words in this portion of Isaiah, 64, which is also the numerical value of the Hebrew word for "prophecy" (נְבוּאָה) and is also the exact number of letters in this final verse that we are analyzing.

The Mystical Symbolism of the Seven Laws of *Bnei Noach*   3

The Nature of the Soul

In order to understand why God gave these seven specific commandments—the Laws of *Bnei Noach*—to all of humanity, we must first briefly explain how the human soul functions.

The human soul has both a Divine and a physical, or animal aspect. In Hebrew these are referred to as the Divine soul (*nefesh Elokit*) and the animal soul (*nefesh behamit*) as defined in the *Tanya*,[1] by the Chassidic Master, Rabbi Shneur Zalman of Liadi.

All human beings possess a Divine spark. The difference between one human and another lies in the extent to which the spark has entered and plays an active role in his or her psyche. (We use the term "psyche" to refer to both the conscious and the unconscious planes of the soul).

When the spark fully enters the psyche[2] it is known as a Divine soul. And so we speak of Jews as possessing a Divine soul. With regard to a non-Jew, the Divine spark hovers above the psyche (not entering it even on the unconscious plane). A righteous gentile (that is, a non-Jew who fulfills the seven Laws of *Bnei Noach*) is one who senses the presence of the Divine spark and is inspired by it to walk along the path of

God fitting for all people as outlined in the Torah.[3] On the other hand, a non-Jew who has not yet become a righteous gentile is unaware of the Divine spark hovering above.

To use the language of Chassidut, the Divine spark (or soul) of a Jew is considered an inner light (*or pnimi*), meaning that it is directly experienced and makes for part of his or her psychological makeup. The righteous gentile's non-Jew's spark of Divinity is described as a "closely surrounding light" (*or makif karov*), meaning that it is psychologically experienced only indirectly. The Divine spark of non-Jews who are not considered righteous gentiles is akin to a "distantly surrounding light" (*or makif rachok*), meaning, that it plays no conscious role in that person's experience as a human being.

Even in this third case, due to the refinement of character that results from life's trials and tribulations, and due to the Divinely ordained meetings between non-Jews and Jews, which introduce the beauty of the Torah to the non-Jew, the "distant" spark may grow "closer" and the "close" spark may even desire to convert to Judaism. It is because of this latent potential innate in every non-Jew that we speak of all non-Jews as possessing a Divine spark. Indeed all of God's creations are continuously brought into being by means of a Divine spark, but, only a human being, even if born a non-Jew, is able to convert in his present lifetime and become a Jew.

These three levels of influence that the Divine spark can have on us as human beings are alluded to in the beginning of the Torah:

> In the beginning God created the heavens and the earth.[4]

In Kabbalah, "the heavens" symbolize the soul and "the earth" symbolizes the body. The Torah continues:

> And the earth was chaotic and void, and darkness
> was on the face of the abyss, and the spirit of God
> hovered over the face of the waters.

The initial state of the earth (the body together with its animal soul) described by the three adjectives "chaotic," "void," and "dark" (which in Kabbalah are identified with the three impure "shells"), corresponds to the initial state of the earthbound non-Jew whose Divine spark is still distant from his psyche. "And the spirit of God hovered over the face of the waters" refers to state of the righteous gentile whose Divine spark is sensed as hovering above him, close to his psyche. The sages teach us that "the spirit of God" refers here to the spirit of the Messiah who will be sent by God to redeem mankind.[5] Thus we may conclude that the coming of the Messiah depends upon raising the spiritual level of the non-Jewish world from "darkness" to "spirit," encouraging non-Jews to become righteous gentiles.

The next verse in the Torah reads:

> And God said: "Let there be light," and there was
> light.

This verse describes the reality of the Jewish soul. "Let there be light" refers to the Divine spark as it permeates the unconscious plane of the Jewish psyche. "And there was light" portrays the Divine spark when it permeates the conscious plane of the Jew's psyche.[6]

Abraham was the first man to integrate the Divine spark as an essential and non-differential part of his psyche (both on the unconscious and the conscious planes). From his inner light he was able to shine light to all around him. In the words of the prophet: "Abraham began to shine light."[7] This made Abraham into the first Jew.

The level to which the Divine spark is present in the psyche has a strong influence on the nature of a person's animal soul. First, let us note that the animal soul is itself divided into two distinct facets, an intellectual facet (*nefesh sichlit*, in Hebrew) and an emotional/behavioral facet. The animal soul of a Jew, due to the inner presence of the Divine soul, is relatively more refined than that of the non-Jew. Its intellectual side possesses a unique Jewish character, or way of thought and reasoning. It is able to grasp abstract and subtle concepts. For this reason Jews are innovative in many secular fields. The passions of its emotional side are directed to things that are permissible according to the law of the Torah.

The physical soul of a righteous gentile resembles that of the Jew in some ways. Consequently, the motivations of the righteous gentile are considered a mixture of good (altruistic) and bad (selfish).[8] However, the state of consciousness of the non-Jew that is not yet righteous, i.e., that is not yet bound to God through the universal aspects of the Torah, conceals and blocks the manifestation of truly good (altruistic) motivations and these cannot be actualized in his physical soul.

When the Divine soul of the Jew is revealed, he or she feels an unconditional love toward all of God's creations, realizing that a spark of God is present in all (with the caveat noted above with regard to the difference between human beings and all other creatures). He or she will love the good in all and reject whatever evil hides, perverts, and corrupts that intrinsic good.

The Soul and the Ten *Sefirot*

We learn in Kabbalah that God created the world through ten *sefirot*—that is through ten emanations of Divine energy. These *sefirot* permeate, and are manifest within every aspect of creation, including, of course, the human soul, which was created in the image of God.[9] Both the physical and the Divine souls are manifest through the *sefirot* and both possess a full array of ten *sefirot*, which, as described in Kabbalah, divide into **three** intellectual faculties and **seven** emotional/behavioral attributes.[10] The three intellectual *sefirot* are wisdom, understanding, and knowledge and are also referred to as "the first three [*sefirot*]" or, the *mochin* (literally, "brains"). The seven emotive *sefirot* are loving-kindness, might, beauty, victory, acknowledgment, foundation, and kingdom and are also referred to as "the lower seven [*sefirot*]" or, the *midot* (attributes).

Nonetheless, relative to one another, the Divine soul is chiefly reflected through the higher **three** intellectual *sefirot*, and the physical/animal aspect is chiefly reflected in the **seven** emotional/behavioral *sefirot*. That is to say that the emotional/behavioral side of the Divine soul is subordinate to (i.e., motivated, directed, and controlled primarily by) its intellectual side, whereas the intellectual side of the physical/animal soul is subordinate to (i.e., serves the interests of) its emotional/behavioral side.

And so, when we speak of the Divine soul as being intellectual in essence and the physical/animal soul as being emotive in essence, we are speaking only of the dominant influence of each soul. For, not only does each soul possess the full array of ten *sefirot*, as described above, but the *sefirot* are wholly inter-inclusive, each containing within it a reflection of all the others. Indeed, one of the most basic teachings of Jewish mysticism is that every complete set of objects possesses the property of inter-inclusion, appearing like a hologram where each element of the set reflects and manifests in itself all of the others.

It is important to note that when we speak of the Divine soul as primarily intellectual, the intellect referred to is the ability of the soul to perceive Divinity directly through the means of the soul's inner, spiritual senses: spiritual sight (wisdom), spiritual hearing (understanding), and spiritual taste (knowledge).[11] Likewise, when we speak of the physical/animal soul as primarily emotive, the two primary emotions of love and fear refer to the love and attraction to that which one feels will bring him or her pleasure and self-gratification and fear and repulsion from that which one feels will be harmful or distasteful. We may thus conclude that the Divine soul is God-oriented, while the physical/animal soul is self-oriented.

Each of the two souls also possesses an eleventh *sefirah* known as the crown, which relates to the super-conscious level of the soul. The soul's crown is the ultimate source of the soul's choice as to which part of its conscious nature (its ten *sefirot* from wisdom to kingdom) will be predominant: its intellectual or its emotive. The crown of the physical/animal soul chooses the self-centered emotive attributes of its soul to be the predominant driving force of the individual's consciousness, whereas the crown of the Divine soul chooses the God-centered intellectual/perceptive faculties to be the predominant driving force of the person's consciousness.

Often in Kabbalah, when enumerating the ten *sefirot*, crown takes the place of the *sefirah* of knowledge. Crown and knowledge are actually reflections of one another, crown in the super-conscious realm of the soul and knowledge in the soul's consciousness. Crown is the unconscious origin of choice, whereas knowledge is the conscious seat of choice.[12]

When crown is counted in place of knowledge, together with wisdom and understanding it becomes part of the group of the intellectual faculties, for in it lies the super-conscious source of wisdom—the place from which the flashes of new insight emerge from the uncharted depths of the soul.

Each of the *sefirot* is given a name describing its unique role in fashioning reality. In addition, the ten *sefirot* are normally pictured as being located on three vertical lines or axes:

- wisdom, loving-kindness, victory, to the right
- understanding, might, acknowledgment, to the left, and
- crown (and knowledge), beauty, foundation, kingdom, down the middle.

All of this information together is depicted graphically in the following arrangement of the *sefirot*, known as the Tree of Life:[13]

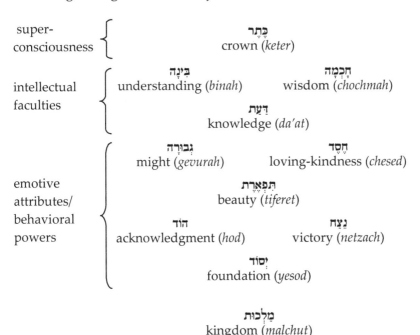

super-consciousness	כֶּתֶר crown (*keter*)
intellectual faculties	בִּינָה חָכְמָה understanding (*binah*) wisdom (*chochmah*) דַּעַת knowledge (*da'at*)
emotive attributes/ behavioral powers	גְּבוּרָה חֶסֶד might (*gevurah*) loving-kindness (*chesed*) תִּפְאֶרֶת beauty (*tiferet*) הוֹד נֵצַח acknowledgment (*hod*) victory (*netzach*) יְסוֹד foundation (*yesod*)

מַלְכוּת
kingdom (*malchut*)

Patterns of 3 and 7

We have seen that the main division of the *sefirot* into the three intellectual and the seven emotional also marks the difference in essence between the Divine and the animal souls. We would like to take some time to deepen our identification of the numbers 3 and 7 and how each represents a different aspect of the sefirotic chart. We do so in order to better understand the place of the seven universal *Bnei Noach* commandments in relation to the rest of the Torah. Clearly, since there are seven universal commandments, mystically they correlate to other instances of seven that are found in the teachings of Kabbalah and Chassidut. Upon carefully examining the chart of the *sefirot*, we will discover two more abstract divisions that configure the *sefirot* into a 3-7 relationship.

To illustrate the first such relationship note that the ten *sefirot* (excluding the eleventh *sefirah* of knowledge, or, were knowledge to be included, excluding crown, as explained above) lie along seven distinct horizontal levels, as in the following diagram:

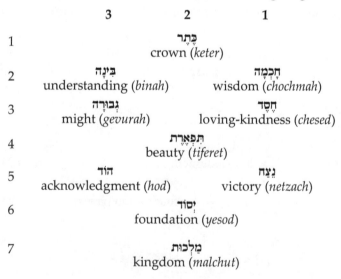

3	2	1
1		כֶּתֶר
		crown (*keter*)
2	בִּינָה	חָכְמָה
	understanding (*binah*)	wisdom (*chochmah*)
3	גְּבוּרָה	חֶסֶד
	might (*gevurah*)	loving-kindness (*chesed*)
4		תִּפְאֶרֶת
		beauty (*tiferet*)
5	הוֹד	נֶצַח
	acknowledgment (*hod*)	victory (*netzach*)
6		יְסוֹד
		foundation (*yesod*)
7		מַלְכוּת
		kingdom (*malchut*)

Coupled with the fact mentioned above that the *sefirot* are also aligned along 3 vertical axes, we have another relationship of 3-7 in the model of the *sefirot*.

In Kabbalah it is explained that the three vertical axes serve to create balance between the *sefirot*. Balance, or equilibrium, is what defines a state of *tikun* (rectification) in Kabbalah.[14] The primordial worlds of *tohu* (chaos) that shattered (the Divinely ordained process referred to as "the breaking of the vessels," mentioned above) were unstable in essence, for their *sefirot* were not aligned in three axes. A stable three-axes alignment of the *sefirot* allows for continual interaction between the *sefirot*. These interactions, or unifications (*yichudim*) as they are called in Kabbalah, sweeten reality by revealing the Divine good inherent in all.

The seven vertical levels correspond to energy levels, energetic rungs of Jacob's ladder reaching upward from earth to heaven. This implies that the number seven relates to ascending or descending through the ten *sefirot* (as did the angels on Jacob's ladder). Though the *sefirot* act in unison, there is still a hierarchical aspect to them whereby crown is higher than wisdom and understanding, and so on. The higher the *sefirah*, the more spiritual its manifestation in reality. Thus, the number 7 reflects the hierarchical ordering of the *sefirot*.

To understand the second 3-7 relationship in the *sefirot* we need to introduce the concept of the conduits (*tzinorot*), or channels, that connect the *sefirot* one to another.[15] Altogether, there are 22 conduits (corresponding to the 22 letters of the Hebrew alphabet), as depicted in the sefirotic chart:

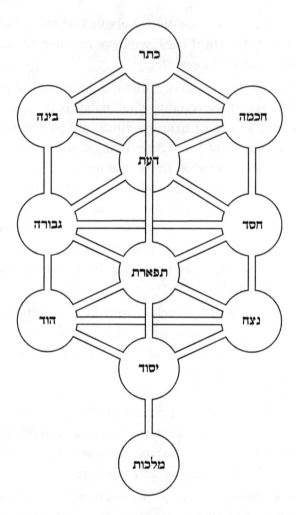

It can be seen that there are three conduits that run horizontally connecting the three *sefirot* on the right axis to the three *sefirot* on the left. There are also, seven vertical conduits that connect *sefirot* that lie along the same vertical axis. (There are also 12 diagonal conduits that do not enter into our present discussion.)

The three horizontal conduits connect, or unite, the left and right axes. The seven vertical conduits connect, or unite, *sefirot* that lie along the same axis. The ability to unite right and left is compared in Jewish mysticism to the quality of a paradox. It is also known as the ability "to sustain opposites," *nesi'at hafachim*[16]).[17] In reference to human nature, the three horizontal conduits are able to unite opposites in the soul, while the seven vertical conduits can only connect manifestations of the same essential spiritual nature of the soul.[18]

Now let us note something more regarding these two 3-7 relationships. In the first, the three are vertical and the seven are horizontal, whereas in the second division the opposite is the case: the three are horizontal and the seven are vertical.

In both 3-7 relationships, the three manifest the powers of rectification, or *tikun*: the three vertical axes of the Tree of Life in the first relationship providing balance and the power to unite the opposites of right and left in the second.[19,20]

The seven horizontal levels permit us to ascend and descend the energy levels of the Tree of Life (the first division). This is a spiritual effort that reflects the soul's proclivity to prefer rising to higher and higher levels of consciousness rather than reaching into and internalizing the Divine essence of the level that it currently occupies. The connecting power of the seven is only between similars (the second division), not between opposites, as noted above.

Finally, we can return to relate all of our above observations to Jewish identity in contrast to non-Jewish identity. The role of the Jewish people in the world, as noted in the introduction, is to be a nation of priests and a light unto the other nations.[21] This function relates primarily to the number three, which refers to:

- the three intellectual *sefirot*,
- the three axes of the rectified (perfectly balanced) Tree of Life, and
- the three horizontal channels that connect the opposites of right and left.

The role of non-Jews in the world (that complements the Jewish role) relates primarily to the number seven referring to:

- the seven emotional/behavioral *sefirot*,
- the seven energy levels of ascent and descent, and
- the seven channels that connect the *sefirot* that lie on the same axis.

For this reason, much of Jewish identity is based on the number three. For example:

- The Jewish people descend from three patriarchs—Abraham, Isaac, and Jacob; indeed in our prayers, we turn to the Almighty as "the God of Abraham, the God of Isaac, and the God of Jacob."[22]
- The Priestly Blessing is composed of three individual blessings: "May God bless you and protect you. May God shine His countenance upon you and be gracious to you. May God turn his countenance toward you and grant you peace."[23]
- The sages state: "Blessed be God, the Merciful One, who gave a three-fold Torah [the Five Books of Moses, the Prophets, and the Writings] to a three-fold people [Priests, Levites, and

Israelites] on the third month [*Sivan*] by means of three [Moses, Aaron, and Miriam]."[24]

Though the principle of three is innate to the Jewish mindset—the Jews' intellectual power—it remains secondary to and is transcended by the Jewish absolute faith in God's essential Oneness. By clinging to the wisdom of the Torah, which links the mind to God, the Divine elements of the soul become fully conscious of the absolute One. It is this truth that Jews seek to impart to non-Jews.

The innate identity of the non-Jew is based on the number seven. For example:

- There are 70 (7 · 10) primal national/ethnic roots, whose origin can be traced to the seventy descendants of Noah enumerated in the Torah.[25]

- The 70 national/ethnic roots relate at their core to the 7 Canaanite nations that occupied the Land of Israel before it was given to the Jewish people by God.[26]

- Between them, the nations communicate using 70 different families of languages.

The number seven (and the number seventy) also has special significance in Jewish tradition. It denotes "endearment." In the words of the sages, "All sevens are dear."[27] For a Jew, the seventh day—*Shabbat*—is qualitatively different from the six weekdays. It is a holy day of rest from worldly endeavor, a time to experience Divine transcendence—God's presence *above* all.

For the non-Jew, on the other hand, the number seven depicts the consummation of secular reality. The seventh day is not essentially different from the other days of the week, it is a workday, and as such, is a time to experience Divine immanence—God's presence *within* all.

Additionally, the number of descendants of Jacob, who were the progenitors of the Jewish people, is explicitly noted in the Torah as seventy.[28] This was also the basis for God instructing Moses to appoint seventy elders[29] to the *Sanhedrin*, the highest court of Torah law.[30] At a deeper level, seventy elders were needed in order to give voice to each of the "seventy facets [faces] of the Torah."[31] Later, the Almighty commanded Moses (who transmitted this directive to Joshua) that upon entering the Land of Israel he was to collect some large stones on which he was to clearly write the text of the entire Torah.[32] The sages explain that God's intent, which was subsequently carried out by Joshua, was that the Torah be translated and written on the stones in all seventy languages of the nations of the world.[33]

This last example of the importance of the number seven in relation to the Jewish people and the Torah is the foundational basis for the task given to the Jewish people to instruct the nations of the world in the ways of God. From this early example of making the entire Torah accessible to every single human being on Earth, without prejudice or pre-condition, we learn that God intended that all people be offered the opportunity to adopt the Torah in full (i.e., convert to Judaism and thereby fully integrating their Divine spark).

The Jewish seven reflects unity—most significantly the Oneness of God—while the non-Jewish seven represents plurality. This is because in the Jewish soul, the seven emotional/behavioral powers are subordinate and serve the spiritual quest of the three intellectual powers (the quest to reveal God's absolute unity). In the yet unrectified state of the non-Jewish soul, the three intellectual powers serve the earthbound desires of the seven emotional/behavioral powers and thus identify at a basic level with the plurality of the mundane.

And so, for the Jewish soul, the quest to ascend (and descend) the seven levels described above remains secondary[34] to its commitment to live a Torah-balanced life, based on the Tree of Life's three axes of right, left, and middle. The right axis corresponds to the soul's commitment to fulfill the Torah's 248 positive commandments, the left axis corresponds to its commitment to fulfill the 365 negative commandments (to refrain from that which the Torah forbids), and the middle axis to the sanctification of all of one's thoughts, words, and deeds, whether in the context of one of the 613 commandments or while involved in one's worldly endeavors.

Likewise, the Jewish soul ideally prefers linking opposites, thereby transcending simple, binary logic, not similars.[35] For the non-Jewish soul, the reverse is the case.

We now return to our initial observation that before committing to the path of the Torah, the non-Jew's intellectual *sefirot* are subordinate to the emotional/behavioral ones. Or, in other words, the non-Jew is innately earthbound. It is exactly to correct this estrangement from all that is Divine and heavenly in nature, that the seven Laws of *Bnei Noach* were given.

A non-Jew that commits to the *Bnei Noach* commandments, experiences a refinement of the seven emotional/behavioral powers within the soul. The individual's physical aspect will begin to serve his or her intellect, and this makes it possible to see through the three uppermost levels of the soul and envision the One.

Simultaneously, by adopting the seven Laws of *Bnei Noach*, the individual reaches the understanding that rectification comes only with subservience to the Torah and as defined by its parameters; this, as opposed to the notion that an untamed desire to ascend spiritually is what brings one closer to God. It is then possible to truly comprehend that God has created a world full of opposites in order that they may consciously be united by all people, thereby revealing God's ultimate Oneness.

When all this happens—and quite often it happens most suddenly—a non-Jew experiences a profound spiritual transformation. But when it does not (and indeed a non-Jew is likely to neglect his or her God-commanded obligations), he or she remains unable to apprehend God's true unity, and is apt to fall into idolatry. This often manifests itself in a distorted worship of some sort—such as the stars, nature, yogis, the pantheon of "gods," money, etc. All are forms of idolatry which can be defined as the worship of *any*thing or *any*one other than the One God. Even the seemingly innocuous modern day movie stars, music stars, and sports stars all contribute to distorting one's ability to commit to worshipping the Almighty.

The Colors of the Rainbow

The number seven is central to the covenant that God made with Noah after the Flood. In this covenant, known as the covenant of Noah, God assured Noah that He would never again destroy the world by water.[36] The visible sign chosen by God to make mankind aware of the covenant was the rainbow.[37]

In Chassidut it is explained that the Flood actually had a purifying effect on the earth and its atmosphere (just as the waters of a ritual bath purify one who immerses in them). Before the Flood, the air was unrefined to the extent that a rainbow could not appear in it. The Flood-waters served to refine the air, allowing for the natural phenomenon of the rainbow to appear.[38]

How many colors are there in the rainbow? According to the *Zohar*,[39] there are three: white, red, and yellow-green! According to Newton, there are seven: violet, indigo, blue, green, yellow, orange, and red. Here, we clearly observe another 3-7 relationship: the inner consciousness and experience of the Divine soul, the context from which the *Zohar* relates, that consciousness experiences three colors in the rainbow. Whereas, the normative, scientific consciousness from where our physical soul relates senses and experiences seven colors in the rainbow. Following our analysis in the first part of this chapter, we may conclude that the Divine soul sees three colors in the rainbow, while our physical soul sees seven!

The Three-colored Rainbow

The first question with regard to the three colors of the *Zohar* is how can white be included as one of the colors? Physically, white does not appear in the rainbow at all! In color theory, the sensation of white is either the result of the color-wheel (with all of its six or seven colors, or more) revolving at a high enough speed so as to make the individual colors imperceptible to the human eye, or the effect of an object reflecting, at once, all of the colors present in the spectrum of the ray of light hitting it. As we shall see, the question of whether white can be treated as a color can only be answered in lieu of the difference between the Divine soul and the physical soul and the way in which each experiences the rainbow.

Like everything else in the world, the colors too correspond to the *sefirot*. The full correspondence is as follows:

	understanding red			wisdom white
		knowledge yellow-green		
	might red			loving-kindness blue
		beauty yellow		
	acknowledgment orange			victory violet
		foundation green		
		kingdom Indigo		

The seven colors observed by the physical soul correspond to the seven lower *sefirot*, the seven attributes of the heart, as described above. The three colors observed by the Divine soul correspond to the three supernal *sefirot*, of which it is said, "The concealed things are for GOD our God."[40] Though they share the same name, the red and the yellow-green perceived by the Divine soul are not the same as those perceived by the physical soul. In addition, even in name, the rainbow's white color remains completely imperceptible to our physical soul.

The *Zohar's* white color of the rainbow refers to the revelation, or the manner in which we might conceptualize what it would be like to see the *sefirah* of wisdom. Wisdom is considered the inner soul of the *sefirah* of loving-kindness, which lies directly under it on the right axis of the Tree of Life. The color associated with loving-kindness is blue and its archetypal soul is Abraham. Correspondingly, Divine wisdom is referred to as the revelation of "the God of Abraham."[41] Divine wisdom refers to the wisdom of the Torah, of which it is said, "He [i.e., the Almighty] and His wisdom are one."[42] In particular, "His wisdom" refers to the origin of wisdom in the wisdom of the super-conscious crown, a faculty that is referred to in the *Zohar* as the "concealed brain" within the will of the soul. Thus, the ultimate origin of the white is in the *sefirah* of crown.

When the *Zohar* refers to red it is actually conceptualizing our intellect's faculty of understanding, i.e., the *sefirah* of understanding. That is to say, that if one were to see the *sefirah* of understanding in one's mind one would describe it as red.[43] Understanding is considered the inner soul of the *sefirah* of might, which lies just under it on the left-axis of the Tree of Life, and which corresponds to the (physical) color red. Again, where the archetypal soul corresponding to might is Isaac, understanding is referred to as the revelation of "the God of Isaac."[44]

The same is true of the *Zohar*'s yellow-green of the rainbow which is the conceptual color of the *sefirah* of knowledge — the inner soul of the *sefirah* of beauty, which lies just under it on the middle axis of the Tree of Life and whose associated color is yellow. As Jacob is the archetypal soul associated with beauty, knowledge is referred to as the revelation of "the God of Jacob."[45]

In the Torah, the word that the *Zohar* uses for "yellow-green" (*yarok*) means either yellow, the color of the *sefirah* of beauty, or green, the color of the *sefirah* of foundation. In Kabbalah, many times the *sefirah* of beauty includes the *sefirah* of foundation,[46] personified by the figure of Joseph, Jacob's son.[47]

Thus, the three colors of the *Zohar*'s rainbow as they correspond with the three *sefirot* that represent the Divine soul are:

understanding	**wisdom**
red	white

knowledge
yellow-green

The Seven-colored Rainbow

As mentioned in the introduction, in the Torah portion[48] that relates the establishment of the covenant between God and Noah (and all generations to come) with the rainbow as the sign of that symbol, the word "covenant" (*brit*) is repeated seven times. These seven appearances of the word "covenant" clearly allude to the seven Newtonian colors of the rainbow, and to the seven Laws of *Bnei Noach*, which, as we shall now see, correspond to the seven emotive/behavioral powers of the soul. The color correspondence is as follows:[49]

	might red		**loving-kindness** blue
		beauty yellow	
acknowledgment orange			**victory** violet
		foundation green	
		kingdom indigo	

Modern physics has revealed that every color is essentially the experience of light particles (photons) traveling at a particular frequency. The physical order of the seven colors as they appear in the rainbow, from higher to lower frequency (from right to left), is: violet, indigo, blue, green, yellow, orange, and red:

(see back cover for figure)

Looking at the rainbow spectrum of colors, the logic behind the correspondence between the *sefirot* and the colors becomes clear. It is a continual left-down and up shift, beginning with victory, the mid-point of the seven *sefirot* of the physical soul. Victory, as will presently be explained, corresponds to the prohibition of idolatry, the most fundamental of all seven Laws of *Bnei Noach*, making it a natural place to start. The full path that we trace is then:

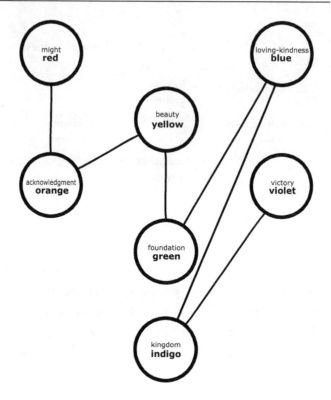

From victory (violet) we move left-down to kingdom (indigo) and then move up to loving-kindness (blue), continuing left-down to foundation (green). We then move up again to beauty (yellow) and then left-down to acknowledgment (orange), finally moving up to might in the upper left corner of the *sefirot*.

The *Sefirot* and the Laws of *Bnei Noach*

In keeping with our recognition of the number seven as specifically related to non-Jews, let us now introduce how the seven Laws of *Bnei Noach* directly correspond to the seven emotive/behavioral powers of the soul which derive from the *sefirot* from loving-kindness to kingdom.[50] Each of the seven

Bnei Noach commandments is meant to guard against the violation or perversion of one of these essential channels of Divine energy:[51]

might	**loving-kindness**
Prohibition against Murder	Prohibition against Adultery

beauty
Prohibition against Theft

acknowledgment	**victory**
Prohibition against Blasphemy	Prohibition against Idolatry

foundation
Prohibition against Eating the Flesh of a Live Animal

kingdom
Injunction to Establish a Just Legal System

Let us begin to explain this correspondence:

That adultery is a perversion of loving-kindness and murder is a perversion of might is obvious.

Theft is a perversion of the *sefirah* of beauty, since beauty as an emotive attribute enables one to relate to another with concern and empathy. The spiritual attribute of beauty desires to manifest in others their own full spectrum of beauty, the spectrum created by themselves together with all of their possessions. The desire and concern that another person's beauty be expressed prevents us from depriving that person of anything that rightfully belongs to him or her. The Torah relates beauty to honor (*kavod*).[52] The sages teach that "Who is honorable? He who honors others,"[53] implying that the spiritual attribute of beauty entails giving honor and showing respect for others. There is no greater lack of respect and consideration than stealing from another person.

True faith in the One God represents the human being's ultimate victory over evil (whose only real power is its ability to misdirect one's faith) and is the gateway to eternity. Thus, idol worship defeats the *sefirah* of victory. Just as the *sefirah* of acknowledgment is the complement[54] of the *sefirah* of victory, so blasphemy, the complement to idol worship is a perversion of the soul's expression of thanksgiving (acknowledgment) to God.

There are two opinions of the sages as to when the sixth *Bnei Noach* commandment, the prohibition to eat limbs amputated from a living animal (*aiver min hachai*), was given to mankind.[55] One opinion is that God gave this commandment to Adam with all the others. Adam and Eve had been instructed by God to be vegetarian, but were forbidden from partaking of the fruit of the Tree of Knowledge: "…for on the day that you eat from it you will surely die."[56] Indeed, for Adam and Eve, the primordial sin itself—eating the forbidden fruit of the Tree of Knowledge of Good and Evil—was comparable to eating a limb torn from a living animal.

In Kabbalah, we learn that had Adam and Eve been patient enough to wait only three hours until the Sabbath eve, the fruit of the Tree of Knowledge would have become permissible.[57] The holiness inherent in the Sabbath would have elevated the spiritual life-force of the Tree of Knowledge, just as ritual slaughtering elevates the life-force of a permissible animal. Eating from the Tree of Knowledge on the Sabbath would have brought with it the blessing of new life (the power to procreate in sanctity, to bring new, holy souls into the world), instead of the penalty of death.

According to another opinion, while the first five and the last of the *Bnei Noach* commandments had already been given to Adam at the outset of creation, the sixth was given to Noah and his children only after the Flood. As noted, Adam and his descendents had been instructed by God to be vegetarian.[58] After the Flood, God permitted Noah—whom the Torah calls the righteous one,[59] the foundation of his generation[60]—to eat animal flesh in general, but forbade him from eating limbs amputated from a living animal.

In the body, the *sefirah* of foundation corresponds to the procreative organ (and thus to sexual arousal). The procreative organ is referred to as the "living limb" (*aiver chai*), a clear allusion to the correspondence of the commandment not to eat limbs amputated from a living animal (*aiver min hachai*) and the *sefirah* of foundation. The spiritual base of this commandment is not to be cruel to living creatures, and, in general, not to be impulsive in one's behavior. The psychological energy inherent in eating a limb torn from a living animal is similar to that which is the basis for an act of rape, the most impulsive of all behaviors. The ability to control oneself and not to succumb to the innate impulsivity of one's animal nature[61] is the power of foundation, as taught in Kabbalah and Chassidut.

The seventh *Bnei Noach* commandment is the only positive one. It is the commandment to establish a legal system in order to judge those who transgress the previous six commandments, and in this way to regulate and rectify society. This commandment corresponds to the *sefirah* of kingdom, for law and order is the basis of any kingdom. As the sages say, "the law of the kingdom is the law to be obeyed."[62]

As we proceed, we will gain further insight into the Kabbalistic logic behind the correspondence just presented.

Note that the first three commandments—the prohibitions against adultery, murder and theft—correspond to the triangle formed by the three primary emotions of the heart, loving-kindness, might, and beauty. These three moral commandments certainly constitute a category unto themselves. The next two commandments—the prohibitions against idolatry and blasphemy—correspond to the integral pair of behaviorist attributes, victory and acknowledgment, known in Kabbalah as "two sides of the body."[63] The next commandment—not to eat limbs amputated from a living animal—corresponds to the *sefirah* of foundation, in a certain sense the most fundamental of all of the Laws of *Bnei Noach*, as will be explained. And so, in logical order, a division of three is followed by a division of two that is followed by a division of one, a general structural phenomenon with regard to the six attributes of the heart.

Finally, the one positive commandment—to establish a just legal system—corresponds to the *sefirah* of kingdom, as explained above. It too, like the commandment that prohibits eating a limb from a live animal, is all-inclusive in nature. But, unlike the singularity of foundation which unifies the preceding *sefirot*, the *sefirah* of kingdom receives and then reflects them all. Likewise, the purpose of establishing just courts of law is to regulate the observance of all the other *Bnei Noach* commandments.

Before the Primordial Sin

Let us add another dimension of depth to our understanding of the spiritual root of the seven Laws of *Bnei Noach*. For this purpose we must expand our vision of the Tree of Life model of the *sefirot*.

We noted that when both crown and knowledge are counted, there are eleven *sefirot*. But in the *Zohar* we find that the crown itself possesses three parts known as the supernal "heads." In the soul, these manifest as super-conscious faith, super-conscious pleasure, and super-conscious will. We now have in all thirteen *sefirot*, with seven along the middle axis.

super-conscious faith

super-conscious pleasure

super-conscious will

understanding   wisdom

knowledge

might   loving-kindness

beauty

acknowledgment   victory

foundation

kingdom

Whereas above we understood the number seven (representative of non-Jewish identity) to be subordinate to the number three (representative of Jewish identity), we now see that from a deeper perspective seven can also be identified with the complete middle axis—the backbone, of the entire Tree of Life (whereas each of the two exterior axes possesses three *sefirot*). Understanding seven in this way clearly far surpasses the previous understanding that linked it with the state of the non-Jewish service of the Almighty.

From this perspective, the seven Laws of *Bnei Noach* take on a new meaning. Before the primordial sin (that resulted in the differentiation between Jewish and non-Jewish soul roots, as explained in Kabbalah[64]) Adam was given seven universal laws in order to emulate God, i.e., to become like God in order to fully actualize the Divine image and likeness in which God created him. Before the primordial sin, the positive side of the *Bnei Noach* prohibitions becomes more pronounced (i.e., the prohibition against idolatry becomes primarily the positive commandment to believe in One God, and so forth). Only with the fall of mankind did these seven laws fall as well from their identification with the seven *sefirot* along the middle pillar of the Tree of Life to the seven lower *sefirot*, for the sake of rectifying the non-Jewish soul.

The original, ideal correspondence of the seven universal laws to the seven *sefirot* along the middle pillar of the Tree of Life is as follows:

Super-conscious faith, the highest of the three heads of the crown, corresponds to the belief in One God and the prohibition against idolatry. Faith is our eternal, unchanging bond to the Almighty, and as such is understood in Kabbalah to be the ultimate origin, in the super-conscious crown, of the *sefirah* of victory/eternity. In the next chapter we will explain that the inner dimension or experience of the *sefirah* of victory/eternity is confidence or trust. Most clearly, the origin of trust is faith.

In Kabbalah, the super-conscious pleasure and super-conscious will of the crown are the origins of the two *sefirot* of loving-kindness and might, and thus correspond to the two commandments prohibiting adultery and murder (whose lower positions in the *sefirot* are loving-kindness and might).

Clearly, adultery is the perversion of the pleasure principle in the soul. Its positive side is to experience life's greatest pleasure in clinging to the Almighty and delving into the mysteries of His Torah.[65] Will is identified in Kabbalah with the flow or running[66] of the blood,[67] the blemish of which is to spill blood.[68] Its positive side is to respect human life, and when seeing another's life in danger, to run to his aid.

In essence, the prohibition against blasphemy is never to show disrespect for the Almighty. For devoted servants of God, as were Adam and Eve before the sin, the subtle origin of disrespect for the Creator (who creates us anew every instant) is to take one's mind off Him, to forget Him and His benevolence to us even for a moment.[69] Thus, the positive side of the prohibition against blasphemy is to always retain consciousness of God. In the soul, this corresponds to the *sefirah* of knowledge (its Hebrew name, *da'at*, can be translated as either "knowledge" or "consciousness"). Always aware of God and His goodness to us, we thank Him in our hearts for the blessings that He continually bestows upon us. And so, the *sefirah* of knowledge is seen to be the origin of the *sefirah* of acknowledgment (the normative position of the prohibition against blasphemy).[70]

The three final commandments—not to steal, not to eat limbs amputated from a living animal, and the establishment of courts of justice—remain in their original positions of beauty, foundation, and kingdom. The positive sides of the first two of these commandments are to respect the property of others (seeing one's property as the beautiful extension, or clothing, of his body) and to respect life in general (foundation in Kabbalah is called *chai*, "life" or "alive"), both human and animal.

super-conscious faith
Prohibition against Idolatry

super-conscious pleasure
Prohibition against Adultery

super-conscious will
Prohibition against Murder

knowledge
Prohibition against Blasphemy

beauty
Prohibition against Theft

foundation
Prohibition against Eating the Flesh of a Live Animal

kingdom
Injunction to Establish a Just Legal System

The Future of *Bnei Noach*

A final point that we would like to address in this chapter is
the future development of those who take it upon themselves
to be *Bnei Noach*—righteous gentiles. Throughout this chapter
we have stressed the relationship between the non-Jewish
nations and the number 7 and between the Jewish people and
the number 3. Interestingly, the Talmud[71] notes that originally,
in the early generations of man, righteous gentiles accepted
not 7, but 30 commandments. The Talmud also notes that the

adherence to these commandments was short-lived and that in practice non-Jews only keep 3 of these 30.[72]

Using our above analysis, we may say that the Talmud is describing an initial attempt of *Bnei Noach* to ascend beyond the realm of Divine emotions (characterized by the number 7) and enter the realm of the Divine intellect (characterized by the number 3 and 30 which is 10 · 3). We may surmise that this initial attempt failed because God had not yet found His chosen people and only through the formation of a bond with them can this elevation be attained. However, as stated in the Jerusalem Talmud, in the future *Bnei Noach* will adhere to all 30 of these laws.[73]

What is the symbolic significance of the elevation from 7 to 30 *Bnei Noach* commandments? Kabbalah and Chassidut explain that the realm of the emotions is where the struggle with evil and chaos takes place (the service of clarification). But, the realm of the intellect is where the determined effort to achieve illumination occurs—not in the sense of the struggle of light against darkness, but rather as the seeking of greater and still greater awareness and consciousness of the Divine everywhere in the world and in our lives (this is called the service of unification). It is explained in Chassidic teachings that the coming of the Messiah heralds the transition from the struggle against evil to the quest for illumination. The era of the Messiah will hit its high mark with the revelation of the World to Come, a world in which human beings will be immortal and everyone's purpose will be to seek greater and deeper understanding of the Almighty.

The sages say that all Jews[74]—and Maimonides adds that all righteous gentiles[75]—have a share in the World to Come, but what might be the relationship between *Bnei Yisrael* and *Bnei*

Noach in this future reality? The answer to this question can be gleaned from a remarkable numerical analysis:

The value of the two statements, "All of Israel have a share in the World to Come,"[76] and "Righteous gentiles have a share in the World to Come,"[77] in the original Hebrew is 2701. This is also the numerical value of the entire first verse of the Torah: "In the beginning God created the heavens and the earth."[78]

In general, the relationship between Jews and righteous gentiles is likened to the relationship between the heavens and the earth. The heavens are relatively more spiritual and conscious of the Divine (like the intellectual *sefirot*, which are symbolized by the number 3), while the earth is relatively more physical and connected to the mundane (like the emotive *sefirot*, which are symbolized by the number 7).

But, regarding the future, the prophet Isaiah says: "Behold, I [God] will create a new heaven and a new earth and the former things will not be remembered nor will they arise upon the heart."[79] In the future, says the Almighty, a new heaven and a new earth will be created, meaning that a new relationship will be formed between the Jewish people and the righteous gentiles. This is the relationship that God had intended from the outset of creation—before the sin of man, which resulted in the fall of the original heavens and earth—as alluded to in the very first verse of the Torah.

With the coming of the Messiah, all worlds—relatively higher worlds symbolized by "heaven" and relatively lower worlds symbolized by "earth"—will ascend to the spiritual level initially intended for them by the Almighty. The "7" of *Bnei Noach* will ascend to "3" and the "3" of *Bnei Yisrael* will ascend to "1." Ultimately, with the continual ascent of the worlds, all *Bnei Noach* will fully convert to Judaism.[80] They will be entrusted with the interpretation of the "body" of the Torah (i.e., the laws of the Torah), likened to "earth," while those Jewish souls who had previously engaged themselves with the study of the Torah's "body" will now immerse themselves totally in the study of the Torah's "soul" (i.e., the inner mysteries of the Torah), likened to "heaven." The heavens will shine their light to the earth and the earth will "ground" the insights of the heavens. And so, all souls will join to manifest God's kingdom and unity in creation.

Notes:

1. Chapters 1 and 2.
2. The spark itself can be likened to a geometrical point, which is dimensionless. After entering the psyche, as the individual develops in his or her commitment to the service of the Divine, the point will expand first to into a line (a one-dimensional figure) and then to an area (a two-dimensional figure). In other words, it becomes more and more real.
3. When a non-Jew becomes so inspired by the spark of Divinity spiritually hovering above that he or she wishes to identify with it in full then that is the true motivation for becoming a convert to Judaism.
4. Genesis 1:1.
5. *Yalkut Shimoni Bereisheet*, 4. According to most Jewish descriptions of the coming of Messiah, particularly the description of Maimonides, the Messiah will be a living Jew, descended from the house of David. He will become king of Israel, rebuild the Temple, and bring all the Jews back to the Holy Land. He will inspire the entire world to believe in the One God, and usher in an era of all human beings living together in peace and brotherhood.
6. These two stages of integration of the Divine spark are alluded to by the sages in the two sayings: "Israel are cherished for they

have been called the sons of the Almighty," and "Israel are cherished for they were the recipients of the precious vessel [the Torah]" (*Avot* 3:14).

7. *Midrash Shemot Rabah* 15:26.

8. See *Tanya*, end of chapter 1.

9. See *Berachot* 10a; *Midrash Vayikra Rabah*, 4; *Midrash Shocher Tov Tehilim*, 103.

10. *Tanya*, chapters 3 and 6.

11. See *The Art of Education*, pp. 106-8.

12. See in depth *Consciousness & Choice*, chapters 1 and 3.

13. For more on this graphical arrangement see *What You Need to Know About Kabbalah*, p. 83.

14. The word *tikun* (תִּקּוּן) in Hebrew is related to the word *kav* (קַו), meaning "line." As described above, the term *kav* refers in Kabbalah to the ray of Divine light that shines into the primordial vacuum created by the *tzimtzum* (the apparent disappearance of God's infinite light, to make room for creation). The *kav* ultimately manifests as the three axes, "lines," of the rectified World of Emanation (the world of *tikun*), with its essence reflected in the middle line of the Tree of Life. This denotes a central tenet of Kabbalah: that only when the *sefirot* are aligned along three axes is it possible to reach a state of rectification. See also *The Hebrew Letters*, p. 61, where the number three represents the qualities of stability and rectification.

15. Altogether there are 22 conduits, which correspond to the 22 letters of the Hebrew alphabet and are divided into 3 groups of 3, 7, and 12 (see *Sefer Yetzirah* 2:1). In our present analysis, the last group of diagonally inclined conduits does not play a direct role.

16. Maimonides, Commentary on the Mishnah, Introduction to Tractate *Avot*, ch. 1. See also *Torah Or* 28c.

17. In Chassidut, the ability to sustain opposites does not diminish from either aspect. Both contradictory qualities remain in their original state.

18. These being the desire to give on the right; the desire to receive on the left; and, the all-important middle axis, which balances the dynamics of giving and receiving.

19. The power to unite opposites is associated with rectification in the *Sifra Detzni'uta* section of the *Zohar* (II, 176b). There the *Zohar* relates this power to the secret of the *matkela* (scale), the property of balance that comes with the division of the *sefirot* into three axes, and explains that this power originates in the inner essence of the *sefirot* that lie along the middle axis, giving them the power to unite right and left.

20. The power inherent in the three axes and in the three horizontal conduits correspond to the final two stages of the three stage process of rectification taught in Chassidut. The three stages are: submission, separation, and sweetening (*Keter Shem Tov*, 28). The three axes correspond to the stage of separation, as they separate the *sefirot* into three headings: right, middle, and left. The power to sustain opposites inherent in the three horizontal conduits corresponds to the stage of sweetening, as the essence of a rectified reality (or faculty of the soul) is that the right unites with the left, thereby sweetening its harsh, judgmental character. For an in depth introduction to this three stage process, see *Transforming Darkness into Light*.

21. Exodus 19:6 and Isaiah 49:6.

22. For example, the opening lines of the *Amidah* prayer.

23. Numbers 6:22-26.

24. *Shabbat* 88a.

25. Genesis chapter 11.

26. Deuteronomy 7:1.

27. *Midrash Vayikra Rabah* 29:11. Chanoch was the seventh generation of mankind, from Adam, whereas Moses was the seventh generation of the Jewish people, from Abraham. Chanoch represents the epitome of a righteous gentile (a potential Jew), and in Kabbalah is seen to be a spiritual mentor of Moses himself!

28. Genesis 46:27 and Exodus 1:5.

29. Numbers 11:16.

30. *Mishnah Sanhedrin* 1:6.

31. *Midrash Rabah Bamidbar* 13:15. See *Ramban's* commentary to Numbers 11:16.

32. Deuteronomy 27:8.

33. *Sotah* 32a. The sages learn this from the word "clearly" in the verse. Kabbalah defines that every word in Hebrew has a "frontside" and a "backside." The frontside is simply the word itself and refers to its literal meaning, while its "backside" is defined as the letters that make up the progressive appearance of the word and refers to its indirect meanings or translations into other languages. How fitting it is that the "backside" of the Hebrew word for "clearly" (הֵיטֵב) is ה הי היט היטב whose numerical value is 70, thus alluding to the seventy languages of the nations into which the Torah was to be translated.

    The numerical value of the "frontside" is 26, the value of God's essential Name, *Havayah*. Multiplying the "front" (26) by the "back" (70) we get 1820, the exact number of times that the Name *Havayah* appears in the Five Books of Moses. Thus, the seventy facets of the Torah that relate to all the nations of the world are themselves illuminated by the power of God's essential Name.

    As noted, the full realization of the vision of the Torah illuminating the entire world only became possible once the Jewish people had entered the Land of Israel. In the Five Books of Moses, the word "clearly" (הֵיטֵב) appears 6 times, the first of which is in the verse, "And You said, 'I will benevolently do you good'" (Genesis 32:13) הֵיטֵב אֵיטִיב עִמָּךְ, which Jacob said to the Almighty referring to the Land of Israel. The Land of Israel is described in the Torah as "the goodly land" that God promised to bestow upon him and his descendants. The two word idiom "I will benevolently do you good" also alludes to this very point, as the product of the numerical values of these two words in

Hebrew is 26 (the value of הֵיטֵב) · 32 (the value of אֵיטִיב) = 832, the numerical value of the "Land of Israel" (אֶרֶץ יִשְׂרָאֵל).

34. When secondary to commitment to live a Torah-balanced life, the quest to ascend (and descend) the sefirotic ladder from rung to rung is positive, reflecting the soul's desire to consciously unite with God. But when the quest to ascend to higher and higher levels of consciousness is one's primary driving force, preceding the commitment to fulfill God's will as revealed in the Torah, it is no other than a reflection of one's base egocentricity. Anything egocentric is essentially earthbound, and though it appears that one is seeking spirituality, in truth one is only seeking self-gratification, on earth.

35. Voicing this sentiment is a well-known Chassidic saying that "you cannot always have the luxury of traveling over an iron bridge." Often, the bridges in life are narrow and flimsy. Nonetheless, the Jewish soul understands that bridges must be constructed and used, even if they do not appear to be ideal.

36. Genesis 8:21. See *Sotah* 11a.

37. Genesis 9:13-16.

38. *Mamarei Admor Hazaken – Bereisheet*, pp. 57-60. The sages list the rainbow among the ten things that were created prior to the rest of creation (*Avot* 5:6). This is learnt from the verse: "My bow I *placed* in the clouds..." (Genesis 9:13), indicating that it indeed did exist before the covenant with Noah (see *Zohar* I, 71b), but it could not be seen as a natural phenomenon until after the flood. See also our upcoming volume on evolution for more insight into this topic.

39. *Zohar* I, 98b.

40. Deuteronomy 29:28.

41. Exodus 3:6, and elsewhere.

42. See chapter 2, note 28.

43. As explained in Chassidut regarding the verse: "your eyes will become red like wine" (Genesis 49:12). The simple meaning is that the pupil of Judah's eye should be as colorful as the color

red, which is the liveliness exhibited by a person drinking wine. Figuratively, this verse depicts the inner understanding symbolized by the color red and perceived by one engaging in meditation, which is symbolized by the drinking of wine. In a similar vein, the sages explain the "when wine enters, secrets are revealed" (*Eiruvin* 65a.). Drinking wine, i.e., meditating on God's Torah, reveals the inner secrets of one's soul.

44. Exodus ibid.

45. Ibid.

46. For "the body [the *sefirah* of beauty] and the procreative organ [the *sefirah* of foundation] are considered one" (*Zohar* III, 223b), unlike the relation of the right arm (loving-kindness) to the right leg (victory) and the left arm (might) to the left leg (acknowledgment), for the leg is not a direct extension of the arm.

47. Jacob and Joseph are also considered one as in the verse: "These are the offspring of Jacob; Joseph…" (Genesis 37:2).

48. Genesis 9:8-17.

49. Often, indigo is not distinguished from violet (victory), and then kingdom is seen to correspond to brown, the color of the earth, created by mixing all the physical colors together, just as the *sefirah* of kingdom receives from all of the *sefirot* above it and possesses no individual color of its own.

50. As we saw above, these seven powers correspond to the seven steps of ascent and to the seven connections of similars of the Tree of Life.

51. In his book, *Gevurot HaShem* (chapter 66), the *Maharal* of Prague (Rabbi Yehudah Leibow, 1512-1609) presents a variant method for corresponding the seven Laws of *Bnei Noach* to a basic Torah model. Though the *Maharal* did not openly employ Kabbalistic terminology in his writings, it is well known that Kabbalistic models and methodology were foundational in the development of his thought and serve as a backdrop for his analyses. For a

presentation of his variant model and its analysis, see our website www.bneinoach.info.

52. Exodus 28:2.

53. *Avot* 4:1.

54. In the human form, the two *sefirot* victory and acknowledgment correspond to the two legs seen as projected from the hips. In the terminology of Kabbalah they are referred to as "two sides of the body" (*Zohar* III, 236a), similar to the idiom "two sides of a coin."

55. *Sanhedrin* 56b ff.

56. Genesis 2:17.

57. *Pri Aitz Chayim, Sha'ar Rosh Hashanah*, chapter 4.

58. Based on the verse: "… From all the trees of the garden you may eat freely" (Genesis 2:16).

59. Genesis 6:9.

60. Based on the verse: "Then GOD said to Noah: …For you alone I have seen to be righteous before Me in this time" (Genesis 7:1).

61. This is especially the case with regard to sexual arousal, which relates in particular to the *sefirah* of foundation. As a youth, Joseph, the archetypal soul of the *sefirah* of foundation, reported to his father Jacob that his brothers were suspected of having eaten limbs torn from living animals (*aiver min hachai*). In order to atone for this, he was tested, later in his life, with regard to sexual arousal. In virtue of his standing the test he merited to be called Joseph the righteous (*Yosef hatzadik*), connoting the rectified power of foundation, as it is said, "The righteous one is the foundation of the world" (Proverbs 10:25).

62. Kingdom receives input from the other powers of the soul, as it is said: "All the rivers [the six emotive powers] flow into the sea [kingdom]" (Ecclesiastes 1:7). In the body, kingdom corresponds to the mouth, whose function is to direct and control society.

63. *Zohar* III, 236a.

64. Arizal, *Sha'ar Hagilgulim*, 7.

65. The holy pleasure of studying the Torah is likened in the Bible to the sanctified pleasure that a man receives from his wife: "…Her breasts shall satisfy you at all times; be exhilarated always with her love" (Proverbs 5:19). This metaphor is further extended to fit our own context when we note that the color of the milk (i.e., the pleasure) received from the Torah is white, the color associated in general with the masculine, right side of the *sefirot*. The super-conscious pleasure of the soul is revealed in the *sefirah* of wisdom as the conscious pleasure derived from the study of the Torah and finds full emotive expression in the *sefirah* of loving-kindness.

66. In Hebrew, the words for "running" and "will" stem from the same two letter root (רצ).

67. Just as milk, which represents permissible pleasure, is white and manifests in the *sefirah* of loving-kindness (see note 65 above), so the red color of blood represents the *sefirah* of might. Impermissible pleasure is represented in the Torah by the choice fat (חֵלֶב) whose color is also white and which in Hebrew is spelled exactly like the word "milk" (חָלָב) but is pronounced differently. Blood can represent either sanctified will—the will to follow God's commandments—or perverse will as in the shedding of blood.

68. One of the verses from which the prohibition to eat flesh from a live animal is glossed is: "Whoever sheds the blood of a man while still in a man, his blood shall be spilt…" (Genesis 9:6).

69. The Ba'al Shem Tov explained that this state of mind is alluded to in Psalms 32:2, which in the original Hebrew can be read: "Blessed is the man for whom not thinking of God is considered a sin…."

70. The letters that make up the name of each letter in the Hebrew alphabet are an acronym for an idiom. The idiom associated with the letter *dalet* (ד, spelled out as דלת) is "Know how to give thanks" (דַע לוֹמַר תוֹדָה, whose initials spell דלת), indicating that the mature consciousness leads the individual to give thanks where thanks is due.

71. *Chulin* 92a.

72. Some later scholars maintain that the 30 are made up of the 7 Laws of *Bnei Noach* we are familiar with in addition to 23 peripheral commandments that derive from them. See Rabbi Menachem Azaria of Pano's *Asarah Ma'amarot, Ma'amar Chikur Din* part III, ch. 21. See also *Sefer Hachinuch*, commandment 416. See also *Talmudic Encyclopedia* s.v. *Ben Noach* (particularly the supplementary article).

73. *Jerusalem Talmud Avodah Zarah* 2:1 (9a).

74. *Mishnah Sanhedrin* 10:1.

75. *Hilchot Teshuvah* 3:5.

76. In Hebrew: כָּל יִשְׂרָאֵל יֵשׁ לָהֶם חֵלֶק לָעוֹלָם הַבָּא = 1298.

77. In Hebrew: חֲסִידֵי אוּמוֹת הָעוֹלָם יֵשׁ לָהֶם חֵלֶק לָעוֹלָם הַבָּא = 1403

78. Genesis 1:1. In Hebrew: בְּרֵאשִׁית בָּרָא אֱלֹהִים אֵת הַשָּׁמַיִם וְאֵת הָאָרֶץ = 2701.

79. Isaiah 65:17.

80. See *Likutei Sichot* v. 23, p. 179, n. 76. As noted there, based on a passage of the Talmud (*Avodah Zarah* 24a), Rabbeinu Nisim, a 14th century Talmudic commentator, argues that indeed all of the nations of the world are destined to convert fully to Judaism (as opposed to merely rejecting their non-monotheistic traditions and beliefs; *Drashot Haran, drush* 7).

One of the most instructive sources about this conversion in stages, i.e., from non-Jew to *Bnei Noach*, to *Gerei Toshav*, to full conversion (*Gerei Tzedek*) is found at the very end of the *Braiyta of Rabbi Eliezer, the son of Rabbi Yosi Hagleelee*. There it is written that every *Ger Toshav*—a *Ben Noach* who has proclaimed his or her commitment to observing the Seven Laws of *Bnei Noach* given by the Almighty—is given 12 months from the time of the proclamation to convert fully to Judaism (i.e., become a *Ger Tzedek*). It may be that, even though not all of the sages agreed with this opinion, the dispute was not about the process, meaning that a *Ger Toshav* is actually an intermediate status in preparation for full conversion, but rather that it may take far more than 12 months. Other sages, as can be understood in the Talmudic passage quoted above, may have argued that this process could take many generations. Nonetheless, the purpose of becoming a *Ben Noach* is to incrementally grow closer to Judaism until full conversion becomes a realistic option, emotionally, and perhaps most importantly, intellectually.

For more Chassidic insight into this topic, see our student Rabbi Yisra'el Ariel's volume *Al Yisra'el Ga'avato*, pp. 55-60 and 202-13.

A Spiritual Path for *Bnei Noach* 4

Revealing the Infinite

To adopt the path of *Bnei Noach*, a person must at the very least follow the seven Laws of *Bnei Noach*. But, like everything in the Torah, the laws contain infinite wisdom and following them marks only the onset of a spiritual path that can carry a non-Jew to find increasing depths of fulfillment in his or her relationship with God. To uncover some of this inner wisdom, in this chapter we will continue to explore the correspondence of the seven Laws of *Bnei Noach* to the seven emotive *sefirot*.

All spirituality and all mysticism originate in faith. A person can live life completely committed to following God's commandments, yet still lack faith in God. This may appear as a lack of belief in God's goodness, or in God's omnipresence, or in God's Providence. Faith and trust are the building blocks out of which every relationship with God is built. Thus, it is essential that *Bnei Noach* know what the faith of *Bnei Noach* entails.

In this chapter we will analyze the seven *Bnei Noach* commandments, which are the legally binding part of the Noahide covenant, and extract from them their spiritual meaning. In the introduction we discussed the 13 Principles of Faith compiled by Maimonides and saw that they may be reduced to 7. Maimonides compiled his list of principles for the purpose of defining halachic, i.e., legal issues regarding the practice of Judaism. Because the halachic standpoint is relatively external when compared with the pure spiritual or inner dimension of the Torah, we may say that the 7 principles of faith derived in the introduction are the vessels that contain the more spiritual principles of faith that we will discuss in this chapter.

Using mystical structures to analyze the commandments of the Torah (whether they be the 613 commandments required from Jews, or the 7 *Bnei Noach* commandments) is the hallmark of contemplative Kabbalah.[1]

Like the 613 commandments of the Torah given to the Jewish people that can be explained as corresponding to the *sefirot*, the 7 *Bnei Noach* commandments also correspond to the *sefirot*. Of course, the correspondence between the 613 commandments and the *sefirot* requires a longer explanation, and due to its complexity is difficult to visualize. But, as we saw in the previous chapter, the seven *Bnei Noach* commandments correspond in a straightforward manner to the seven lower *sefirot*.

The Inner Dimension of the Laws of *Bnei Noach*

In this chapter we will focus on the more spiritual, inner meaning of each of the seven *Bnei Noach* commandments. To uncover each commandment's inner meaning, we need to understand the inner dimension of the *sefirah* to which it corresponds.

Each of the seven powers of the soul, which emanate from the *sefirot* (as explained earlier) also has an inner dimension. Whereas the external dimension of each *sefirah* describes the functional role that the *sefirah* plays in the process of creation, its inner dimension describes the hidden or underlying motivational force that inspires its role.

Another way of describing this relationship is that the outer dimension of the *sefirah* focuses on the vessels of creation, while the inner dimension focuses on the lights that fill these vessels.[2] Vessels serve to reveal and channel the lights. Without the vessels, the lights would remain hidden or unconscious. Thus, the lights need the vessels in order to affect reality. When the vessels are void of light they are likened to a body without a soul giving it life and inspiration. Both are necessary and each complements the other. God desires that in our Divine service both vessels and lights manifest simultaneously.

Vessels are created when we perform a God-given commandment by means of one of the external powers of the soul. The performance of a Divine commandment may require either proactive involvement or conscious resolve to restrain from that which is forbidden.

However, most people find it difficult to perceive the spiritual aspect of the performance of commandments. The spirituality inherent in the Torah's commandments can be experienced through meditation upon the spiritual hue of the Divine life-force manifest in the performance of each particular commandment, i.e., the light contained within the vessel. The light may be of the nature of life-giving love or fear or one of the other attributes of the heart. Experiencing the inner aspect of each commandment allows us to experience in our soul the inner dimension of the Divine reality that is everywhere present in order to serve our Creator in accordance with His Will.

The inner dimensions of the *sefirot* correspond to the powers of the soul and the seven Laws of *Bnei Noach* as follows:

might	loving-kindness
fear	**love**
Prohibition against Murder	Prohibition against Adultery

beauty
mercy
Prohibition against Theft

acknowledgment	victory
sincerity	**confidence**
Prohibition against Blasphemy	Prohibition against Idolatry

foundation
truth/fulfillment
Prohibition against Eating the Flesh of a Live Animal

kingdom
humility
Injunction to Establish a Just Legal System

Examining the seven Laws of *Bnei Noach* in this manner allows us to identify seven principles of Divine meditation and service, whose purpose is to inspire and direct the lives of *Bnei Noach*. Each of these principles corresponds to the experiential and motivational factors that go into each of the seven Laws of *Bnei Noach*. It is to these that we now turn our attention, but let us first chart the full correspondence between the *sefirot* and their inner dimension and the seven *Bnei Noach* commandments and the seven principles of Divine meditation that we will be introducing:

might
fear
Prohibition against Murder
Standing in Awe Before God

loving-kindness
love
Prohibition against Adultery
Continual Recreation of Reality

beauty
mercy
Prohibition against Theft
Recognizing God's Miracles

acknowledgment
sincerity
Prohibition against Blasphemy
Becoming a Servant of God

victory
confidence
Prohibition against Idolatry
Committing to Self-transformation

foundation
truth/fulfillment
Prohibition against Eating the Flesh of a Live Animal
Experiencing Divine Providence

kingdom
humility
Injunction to Establish a Just Legal System
Making a Home for God on Earth

Loving-kindness: Experiencing Continual Re-creation

Love is the essential power of spiritual growth inherent throughout reality. God created the world with love and sustains it through love. The experience of love between two people, a man and a woman,[3] begins with a sense of attraction—a feeling that continues to grow and expand until it encompasses one and one's beloved in marital union. It is easy to see how adultery, which violates this bond, is a terrible transgression against love. Therefore, the prohibition against adultery is an antidote to the perversion of the power of loving-kindness and of its inner dimension—love.

From this observation, we derive the first principle of Divine meditation and the beginning of the *Bnei Noach's* rectification process and service of the Almighty: the recognition that God continually re-creates the universe with love.

It does not require superhuman intelligence to realize that God created the universe. No entity creates itself. However, the human mind is time-bound, and even if it is convinced that the world was created ex-nihilo (perhaps by way of a Big Bang or some similar process), the act of creation appears to have occurred in the remote past. From that moment on, it seems as though the universe has evolved naturally; its total amount of energy and matter has remained fixed, and only its forms have undergone change. To human perception, it seems that there is no new input of energy into the universe now.

And yet the Torah teaches us that this is not the case.

Consciousness of God the Creator begins with the recognition that God is not time-bound and that He recreates the world anew in each instant. Were God not actively involved, as it were, in continual re-creation, the entire universe would revert to primordial nothingness.[4]

In order to understand and grasp the notion of continual re-creation we must begin by experiencing the infinite love felt by God for each and every created being. And so the Psalms teach: "The world is built from loving-kindness."[5] Both originally, and at every subsequent moment, the world is dependent on a constant influx of God's love for creation.

We might wonder why continual recreation is not openly observable. Why is it that it can only be experienced through meditation? Chassidic teachings explain that there is an inherent measure of modesty, or intimacy in the creative act.

We can see this by comparing it with the act of pro*creation* in human beings. Just as in the holy union of marriage, the gift of vital seed is given in complete modesty, so it is when God re-creates the universe at every moment.

In our comparison, the husband symbolizes God the Creator and the wife symbolizes creation. The vital seed is the Divine power of re-creation. The modesty of the holy union of husband and wife symbolizes God's (*conscious*) will to create the world (together with the world's *unconscious* will to be created by God) in such a manner that the normative consciousness of creation remains unaware of the Divine act of continual re-creation. God desires that the wonder of continual re-creation be known only to the loving, attentive, and meditative eye of those souls that truthfully search for Him.

Let us take a deeper look at the relationship between the continual recreation of reality and love. The archetypal soul in the Torah that personifies the attribute of love is Abraham. The letters of his name in Hebrew (אַבְרָהָם) permute to spell the Hebrew word for "creation" (הִבָּרְאָם) as it appears in the first verse of the second account of creation in the Torah.[6] The sages interpret this phenomenon to mean that God created (and continuously re-creates[7]) the world with the power of the Divine soul-root of Abraham, the power of love.[8]

Non-Jews who recognize that their very existence and the existence of all created reality is continually dependent upon God's infinite love—which in essence is identical with the soul-root of the first Jew, Abraham—are drawn in love to the Jewish people. Some will remain righteous gentiles and abide by the seven Laws of *Bnei Noach,* and some will undergo full conversion to Judaism.

Of Abraham, together with his wife Sarah, it is said that they made, i.e., created the souls of righteous converts during the time that they had marital relations but did not conceive physical children.[9] In their great love for one another—each experiencing in the other a reflection of God—and in the complete modesty of their holy marital union,[10] they became partners with God in the act of continual re-creation.

The word "create" in Hebrew (*bara*) is closely related to the word for "healthy" (*bari*). As God continually re-creates the universe, He continually heals its wounds.[11] To be aware of continual re-creation is to draw Divine healing power into one's being. Such awareness, whether for the Jew or the non-Jew, heals and gives one the power to heal others. Indeed, it was Abraham,[12] the very embodiment of the power of love, who first healed others through prayer to God.[13]

Might: Standing in Awe of God

In contrast to the heart's initial desire to reach out and give, which derives from love, fear evokes the strength of character necessary to reject and fight off destructive forces. Many times this is necessary but more often than not our fears have no real basis and can turn us into a destructive force ourselves.

Chassidut explains that our fears need to be sublimated. In its most abstract sense fear is related to sensitivity to others, in general. When not in the context of a need to repel a threatening, dangerous other this sensitivity has to motivate us to be considerate of other people's feelings and to respect them. When fear is sublimated it yields a concern for hurting other people's feelings or causing them injury in any way. To rectify our fears and turn them into care and sensitivity we need to meditate on the experience of fear in its rectified form in the Torah.

In the Torah, the attribute of fear is associated with the second patriarch of Israel, Isaac, the archetypal soul of the *sefirah* of might, whose consciousness of God is referred to as "the Fear of Isaac."[14] Meditating on fear as the quality of Isaac's worship of the Almighty sublimates it in ourselves.

Again, unrectified fear that remains in its initial raw state, misdirects one to fear men instead of God and eventually becomes the motivation for acts of violence and ultimately murder. This was the trait of Isaac's son Esau, whom his father blessed with the words, "And you shall live by your sword."[15]

The crime of murder is the most violent expression of insensitivity and lack of respect for another. Furthermore, it indicates that visibly the transgressor fears no-one, not even the Almighty. Therefore, the prohibition against murder guards against the worst possible violation of the power of might and of its inner experience of fear.

From this we derive the second principle of Divine meditation and service for *Bnei Noach*: the fear/awe of God.

All human beings possess free will, and indeed non-Jews can exercise their free will to either observe or ignore the seven Laws of *Bnei Noach*. But in a deeper sense, for both the Jew and non-Jew, there is only one choice to be made—whether or not in this moment of life to turn to God in submission to His Will. This is encapsulated in the saying of the sages, "all is in the hands of Heaven except for the fear of Heaven."[16]

In a sense, this precept especially pertains to the Divine service of the non-Jew. There are two similar verses in Psalms that begin with the phrase, "Serve God...." One reads: "Serve

God in joy."[17] The other reads: "Serve God in fear."[18] The sages interpret the verse "Serve God in joy" as addressing Jews, in particular and the verse, "Serve God in fear" as addressing non-Jews, in particular.[19] Of course, both Jews and non-Jews must serve God with both joy and fear/awe—the only difference is the emphasis.

Additionally, there are many levels of fear or awe of God. For non-Jews, the most basic level—the one which motivates refraining from sin—is *fear* of punishment.[20] For Jews, the *sefirah* of might translates first and foremost as the *awe* of God as the omnipotent Ruler of the universe. Whereas both *fear* and *awe* relate to God's power to decree life or death, the first does not focus on the Almighty King Himself, but solely on the threat of His punishment. Human *fear* of Divine judgment evolves from the baser animal fear of imminent danger. But, *awe* is a more refined emotion that derives from a higher experience of the Divine. *Awe* is the experience of standing in front of the King Himself, in all of His majesty—not in front of His judgment. Awe is thus an experience distinct to the higher faculties of man. By identifying with the way of the Torah (which was given to all of mankind) and keeping the seven Laws of *Bnei Noach*, non-Jews may also experience *awe* of the Almighty King Himself, not just of His judgment.

As stated, no matter what the motivation, ultimately, the one and only choice that a person truly makes in life is whether or not to turn to God. The Jew turns to God in love and serves Him with joy. His awe of God is present within the joyful experience of standing before Him in service.[21] The non-Jew, inspired by the Torah, turns to God in awe.[22]

∞

In the Bible, the most profound account of a non-Jewish society turning to God is that of the repentance of the city of Nineveh, recorded in the Book of Jonah. Jews read this story at the high point of the holiest day of the year, Yom Kipur—the Day of Atonement.

The prophet Jonah is commanded by God to pronounce judgment on the residents of Ninveh. Attempting to evade his mission, Jonah flees aboard a ship, but he cannot escape— during his journey, a terrible storm is sent by God. A lot is cast by the non-Jewish sailors to reveal who is to blame for the storm and it falls on Jonah. He tells the sailors that he is fleeing from God, and, after turning to God in prayer, they throw Jonah overboard and he is swallowed up by a large fish. Eventually, Jonah acquiesces to God's command, and the fish spits him out. He arrives in Ninveh where he proclaims God's judgment. Quaking in fear of their impending punishment, the residents begin a penitent fast and turn back from their evil ways.

In this story, we see that it was Jonah, a Jewish soul, who became a tool in the hands of God to arouse a multitude of non-Jewish souls to turn to Him in sincere repentance. Initially, it appears from the text that the inhabitants of Nineveh were motivated by their *fear* of punishment. However, a deeper reading of the text reveals that their sudden transformation was the result of being inspired by Jonah and his own miracle at sea. Just as Jonah's awe of the Almighty had caused him to acquiesce to God's Will, they too experienced a sense of *awe* of the God of Israel and became an example of repentance to others.

The emotion of fear is clearly the opposite of the emotion of love. From the final verse of the Book of Jonah we learn that an inability to experience the awe of God is a sign of psychological immaturity. The verse reads: "Should I [God] not have compassion on the great city of Ninveh, which contains more than 120,000 people who cannot discern between their right-hand and their left-hand, and myriad animals" (Jonah 4:11). According to the commentaries, "people who cannot discern between their right-hand and their left-hand" refers to immature youths. Chassidic teachings elaborate that the inability to distinguish between right and left hands describes (even older) individuals for whom love (the Divine service symbolized by the right hand) and fear (the Divine service symbolized by the left hand) are not yet well defined. In other words, these individuals are unable to fully distinguish love from fear, as neither their love nor their fear are mature and independent of one another. Only when innate opposites (such as male and female) mature in full are they able to complement one another, function in partnership, and unite. Serving God with mature love allows the individual to simultaneously include the experience of awe of God (symbolized by the left hand) within the experience of the love and joy of serving God (symbolized by the right hand).

Still, even those individuals referred to as unable to discern between the right hand and the left hand are capable of experiencing a certain measure of awe of the Almighty King. But, "myriad animals" (which the commentaries say also refers to a certain class of human beings[23]) refers to those individuals who can only experience a base fear of punishment.

The distinction just described between youth and "the myriad animals" can help us understand an important rule of education. Namely, that even a child is capable of grasping the meaning of awe before God and should be taught to stand in awe in the Presence of God, and not to solely fear punishment.

From the time of the Ba'al Shem Tov, the founder of the Chassidic movement, fear of punishment has been sublimated. In a certain sense, it has gone "out of style,"[24] as the Ba'al Shem Tov's teachings (and the light that he and his disciples shined to the world, whether consciously recognized and acknowledged or not) serve to elevate even the most simple of people, whether Jewish or not, to a higher level of consciousness. Indeed, the primary emotions that people now experience in relation to the Almighty are love and awe. Awe, unlike fear, is accompanied by a sense of wonder that one experiences when witnessing God's handiwork in creation. Maimonides explains that by observing nature, by experiencing the wonder of nature revealing its Creator, a person comes to develop both the love and the fear (as awe) of the Almighty.[25]

Beauty: Recognizing God's Miracles

Mercy, the inner dimension and experience of beauty, the third of the emotive attributes, synthesizes the two previous, opposing emotions of love and fear. The archetypal soul of the *sefirah* of beauty was Jacob, who as the third patriarch of Israel, synthesized the two levels of Divine consciousness personified by his grandfather and father, Abraham and Isaac. Mercy is the sense of true empathy with another soul in its present life situation. When one judges another with mercy, one sees beyond superficiality and finds worthiness in the other's essence.

In our prayers (especially on the High Holidays, the days of judgment), we beseech God, in judging the world, to stand up from His throne of severe judgment (*kisei din*) and sit on His throne of mercy (*kisei rachamim*).[26] When Jacob sent his sons for the second time to Egypt to purchase grain, he prayed for their success with the words: "May the Almighty God give you mercy."[27]

Theft is a perversion of the power of beauty, as explained above. Thus, theft is also a crime against the inner dimension of beauty—mercy. Chassidut explains that God's mercy is revealed by the miracles that He performs.[28] We can now derive the third principle of Divine meditation and service for *Bnei Noach*: awareness of God's miracles in our lives.

Ironically, thieves live on miracles. As observed by the Chassidic masters, thieves place themselves in danger, relying on a miracle to steal without getting caught. In fact, they even pray to God, whether consciously or unconsciously, to help them steal, all this while, paradoxically, totally disobeying His Will.[29]

At the outset of creation, God saw that if He created a universe in which each individual is judged exactly in accordance with the merit of his deeds and intentions, the universe would not persist. He therefore combined (severe) judgment with mercy, and created the world with both.[30] God's mercy extends to all His creations, as is said in Psalms: "God is good to all, and His mercy extends to all His creatures."[31] Thus, in the end, the natural order of creation reflects Divine judgment, while miracles (defined as acts that supersede the strict laws of nature, which do not seem to distinguish between individuals) express Divine mercy.[32]

In practice, because these three: loving-kindness, judgment, and mercy are separate *sefirot*, each can be experienced separately or in unison. The experience of continual re-creation is the experience of Divine loving-kindness, the first of the emotions of the heart. The experience of the lawfulness and order in nature, which function within the limits of created time and space, is the experience of Divine might and judgment.[33] Experiencing miracles is to experience God's infinite mercy—the third, synthesizing, emotive force. Through His attribute of mercy God is less exacting with us and allows the supernatural realm to manifest freely within the natural. In Kabbalah and Chassidut, we are taught that these first three emotive forces flow naturally, one following the other.[34]

Recognizing God's mercy as revealed through miracles[35] arouses a desire in the human heart to turn to God in devoted worship. Recognizing God's miracles at work in the world means recognizing His desire and power to change the course of nature not just in response and in proportion to the merits of human beings, as is the function of Divine judgment. The sages refer to prayer as "[beseeching] mercy" (rachamei).[36] We pray that God miraculously heal the sick, provide for the poor, and bless the barren with children. We pray for the clarity of mind and heart to know God, and to be able to emulate His ways. The sages teach us that the way to arouse God's mercy is to emulate His attribute of mercy, to empathize with others, and to shower compassion upon them. They promise: "Whoever shows mercy to others will be shown mercy from Heaven."[37]

By contemplating history, both past and present, non-Jews will surely see the wonder of God's mercy on His chosen people as he blesses them with countless miracles.[38] Even in times of destruction and exile, the flame of the Jewish people has never been extinguished (as the laws of nature would seem to have dictated). By contemplating this phenomenon, non-Jews connect to the Divine attribute of mercy in their worship of God.

In our prayers we allude to the Messiah who will bring salvation to the entire world as "a beggar beseeching mercy at the doorstep."[39] By recognizing God's attribute and deeds of mercy for all (and especially His mercy and miracles on Israel), non-Jews are also able to connect to the soul of the true savior of humanity.

Victory: Committing to Self-transformation

Trust, the inner dimension and experience of the *sefirah* of victory, begins with the assurance that everything that Divine Providence brings about in this world is for the good. In truth, all is good, but not all of God's good is visible to our eyes; some is concealed in the garb of evil. But this garb is temporary, and when removed (sooner or later) the kernel of good will be revealed and it will become clear that even the temporary appearance of evil was for the sake of the eternal good. And so we may say that in essence all is good, for all is from God who is the essence of good, but to our eyes, all is, at least, *for* the good.

Trust is also evident in feeling confident that God is always with me, standing at my side to help me overcome life's obstacles, and giving me the power and resources necessary to accomplish life's goals. Thus, by trusting and having confidence in God alone, I can acquire a rectified state of self-confidence.

Idol worship—which translates into a dependency on anything other than the One God—undermines one's trust in God, in the trust that all comes from God and that all is good.

Trust that all is good—even in the face of evil—represents the ultimate victory over that very evil and is the gateway to eternity. Therefore, the prohibition against idolatry safeguards against the perversion of the *sefirah* of victory and its inner dimension—trust. Trust in the essential good of the Almighty leads us to believe in the power of self-transformation.

Thus, the commitment to constantly battle one's evil inclination in order to undergo a process of self-transformation constitutes the fourth principle of Divine meditation and service for *Bnei Noach*.

In serving God, the ultimate victory in the human soul is the triumph of one's good inclination over one's evil inclination. To the extent that one is victorious in this spiritual battle, one merits a metamorphosis of being. On the other hand, idolatry, which is deterministic in essence, does not allow for the possibility of spiritual metamorphosis.[40]

Though the Torah does not suggest that all non-Jews convert to Judaism, it does require that they undergo a type of semi-conversion[41] in order to become righteous gentiles. During this semi-conversion, non-Jews accept upon themselves the seven Laws of *Bnei Noach* as given to mankind in the Torah, thus recognizing the authority of the Torah over their lives. Thereby, they become transformed and acquire a greater level of free will than that which they possessed previously. Once they do so, they are regarded in a most special way in Jewish law. Indeed, the Torah itself attaches great importance to righteous gentiles. It commands the Jewish people not only to accept them as resident aliens (*gairim toshavim*) in the Land of Israel, but to provide for their welfare.[42]

As noted, the inner dimension of victory—trust in God—produces a sense of self-confidence born of the realization that God continuously provides every individual with the spiritual resources necessary to rectify his or her behavior and character traits, and thus transform himself or herself into a truly new being.

∞

Victory is the extension of loving-kindness on the right axis of the Tree of Life. In Divine service, loving-kindness corresponds to the consciousness of continual re-creation (as described above). Victory and self-transformation are made possible by the sense that just as God re-creates the world every moment, so too, each human being may rectify and transform himself or herself every moment—it is never too late and everything is possible. God gives each and every human the power to re-create himself.

Creation is an ex-nihilo act of the Creator. In Hebrew, "something from nothing" is called *yesh mai'ayin*. In order to be re-created one must first return to a state of nothingness (*ayin*), from which a new state of somethingness (*yesh*) can emerge. Using the imagery of Chassidut, only after the seed that fell from the previous life-form rots in the ground can a new life-form sprout from the earth. The potential for new life was present in the past, but it itself must return to nothingness in order for new life to emerge.

The greatest souls—like Moses and the Ba'al Shem Tov[43]—are those *tzadikim* that experience personal re-creation/metamorphosis every moment of their lives.[44] They thereby become conduits to draw Divine creative power into the world, and to create things anew, even in the external dimension of reality.[45] Moses—the archetypal soul of the *sefirah* of victory—created[46] a "mouth" for the earth to swallow up Korach and his congregation.[47] The Ba'al Shem Tov would light an icicle, like a candle,[48] when he needed to immerse at night in a frozen river.[49] Even though we cannot compare ourselves to Moses or to the Ba'al Shem Tov, we can and should receive inspiration from them, and know that we too can transform ourselves (and those aspects of reality necessary for our service of God) into new beings.

Victory follows the three previous emotive attributes—love, fear/awe, and mercy. After experiencing God's love, one turns to Him in awe (the hallmark of manifest free will), and comes to recognize His mercy. The greatest miracle wrought by God upon humanity is the gift of the potential to transform oneself into a truly new being (the attribute of victory).[50]

As noted, here too non-Jews take their lead from the Jews, the nation of priests (and especially from the great leaders of Israel, like Moses and the Ba'al Shem Tov). Victory for Jews entails the climbing of the levels inherent in the physical aspect of their soul, and the merging of these levels with the energy source of the Divine aspect of their soul (as described at length in the previous chapter).

Initially, the physical aspect of the Jewish soul comes from what is referred to in Kabbalah as the intermediate shell[51]— that state of being which possesses a mixture of good and evil. In Hebrew, the name of this intermediate shell is *nogah*, which literally means a "glow." It indeed possesses an element of Divine glow, which reflects its inherent good, but its glow is not clear and brilliant.

When non-Jews undergo the semi-conversion process necessary for becoming righteous gentiles, they ascend from their spiritual imprisonment to become identified with the glowing intermediate shell. In this way, they are similar to the Jews who have not yet undergone the rectification process described above. It is for this reason, that the Jewish nation is commanded to sustain the righteous gentiles (both physically and spiritually), thereby endowing them with the power to continue to overcome the negativity inherent in the intermediate shell (so that its good be able to overcome its evil). Were they to fully convert to Judaism, righteous gentiles would continue their ascent toward the Divine energy source along with the Nation of Israel, acquiring the Divine soul of Israel itself.

Acknowledgment: Becoming a Servant of God

Sincerity (*temimut*) is the inner experience of the *sefirah* of acknowledgment (or thanksgiving, as it is sometimes translated). The word for sincerity in Hebrew also implies completeness[52] and simplicity.[53] At the level of the super-conscious, sincerity represents one's singular will dedicated to fulfilling God's Will. In the heart, sincerity represents one's earnest intent to serve God with devotion. When manifest in action, sincerity promises that one will be committed to fulfilling each and every detail of God's commandments.[54] With a sincere and simple character, one seeks to fulfill God's Will with love and gratitude.

Blasphemy—a contemptuous act or utterance concerning God—perverts the soul's naturally sincere expression of thanks to God and acknowledgment of God's infinite goodness and grandeur. Therefore, the prohibition against blasphemy protects the psyche's *sefirah* of acknowledgment and its inner dimension—sincerity, and from it derives the fifth principle of Divine meditation and service for *Bnei Noach*—becoming a sincere servant of God and His chosen people, Israel.

The Torah calls *Bnei Yisrael*, en masse, "the son of God": "Thus said God, 'Israel is My son, My firstborn.'"[55] *Bnei Noach*, on the other hand, are ideally likened to the servants of God. When *Bnei Yisrael* do not manifest the essence of their Divine soul—"an actual part of God,"[56] as son to father—they are also referred to as a servant.[57] Though in relation to Jewish consciousness this is definitely a shortfall, in relation to creation as a whole, it serves a positive purpose.[58] As we have seen, it is the responsibility of the Jew to show the non-Jew how to worship God. When a Jew serves God as a servant, he inspires the non-Jew to rise to the same level, and thus to become himself a servant of God.

Service, or worship is identified in Kabbalah with sincerity. A sincere individual can stand before his master in total submission of self and absolute commitment of will. This sincere state of submission creates an aura that encompasses both master and servant. An additional meaning of the Hebrew name of the *sefirah* of acknowledgment, *hod*, is indeed "aura."

The *sefirah* of acknowledgment and its inner experience, sincerity, lie at the very end of the left axis of the Tree of Life. *Sefirot* that lie along the same axis, among other things share a hierarchical-like relationship. On the left axis, understanding is considered the origin, or the highest *sefirah*, while acknowledgment is considered the terminal, or lowest *sefirah*. Thus, submission and commitment, which we have seen are associated with the *sefirah* of acknowledgment are considered the extension of the *sefirah* of might and its inner experience of fear, or awe. What this means in practice is that when non-Jews learn submission and commitment from Jews, they can ascend from acknowledgment to might, thus meriting to serve God with awe. Likewise, the *sefirah* of might acts as an extension of understanding. In practice, this means that by devotedly supporting the Jewish people and helping them to succeed in their special mission of bringing Divine light to the world, non-Jews merit to serve God with joy, which is the inner experience of the *sefirah* of understanding.

When in the presence of his Master, the sincere and simple servant's heart is filled with awe. But, at the same time, deep in his heart, the loyal servant rejoices in the privilege of devotedly serving his Master. For a non-Jew, the experience of this privilege can be felt most when there is a commitment to help and serve the Jewish people, the sons of the Master.

As explained earlier, victory and acknowledgment—trust and sincerity—complement one another. These two *sefirot* represent two aspects of the process of becoming a righteous gentile. From victory comes the trust needed to accept the seven Laws of *Bnei Noach* and to take the lead from the Jewish people that it is possible to spiritually transform and reach a higher level of being. Acknowledgment establishes a sincere commitment to serve God and deepens one's awareness that to become a trustworthy servant of God requires an equally sincere commitment to the well-being of the Jewish people—God's firstborn.

The archetypal souls that correspond to victory and acknowledgment—Moses and his brother Aaron—are also central to the process of becoming a righteous gentile. The Zohar[59] teaches that in the Divine marriage between God and His chosen people, the children of Israel, Moses assumes the role of the groom's consort and Aaron assumes the role of the bride's consort. Moses acts on behalf of God (the groom) by bringing God's essence to the consciousness of the people and teaching them how to know God. Aaron escorts the Jewish people (the bride) to the wedding canopy—i.e., their unification with the Almighty—by igniting their souls to love God with the all-encompassing commitment and intense passion that a bride has for her groom. Identifying with the figure of Moses, the archetypal soul of victory and the giver of the Torah, awakens the non-Jew's willingness to commit to the Laws of Bnei Noach that are a part of the Torah. Identifying with Aaron, the archetypal soul of acknowledgment who, in his role as the high priest, embodies the highest level of Divine service, helps the non Jew to commit to the well-being of the Jewish people—supporting and encouraging them to consummate their relationship with God, for the ultimate sake of bringing peace and redemption to the world, of giving birth to a new world order.[60]

The Hebrew word for "Jew," *yehudi*, stems from the Hebrew name of the *sefirah* of acknowledgment, *hod*. This implies that a Jew is one who acknowledges God unconditionally, accepting His infinite greatness and giving thanks to Him for all that befalls him in life, regardless of whether the good is plainly apparent, or not.

A non-Jew can also strive to manifest the characteristic properties of the *sefirah* of acknowledgment. To fully identify with spiritual acknowledgment and sincerity a *Ben* or *Bat Noach* must complete the semi-conversion process and become a righteous gentile. This includes not only accepting the seven Laws of *Bnei Noach* but also acknowledging the unique role of the Jewish people and the dependence of all mankind on them succeeding in their mission. This realization motivates the righteous gentile to do all in his power to aid God's chosen people in their Divinely ordained role.

The classic example in the Torah of a gentile servant who merited to manifest acknowledgment in this manner was Eliezer, the Canaanite servant of Abraham. Due to his total dedication to his master, Abraham placed him in charge of his entire household. He was also given the responsibility of finding a wife for Abraham's son, Isaac. In his sincere and absolute devotion to the will of Abraham, Eliezer merited to undergo spiritual metamorphosis, to leave the realm of the cursed and enter the realm of the blessed.[61] This was as God had promised Abraham: "I will bless those who bless you and curse those who curse you."[62]

When identifying himself to Bethuel, Rebecca's father, and to her brother Laban, Eliezer did not say "I am Eliezer, Abraham's servant," but rather simply proclaimed: "I am Abraham's servant."[63] He did not refer to himself by his proper name, only by Abraham's, for he had reached such a level of devotion to his master, that he no longer possessed an independent identity. He had reached the true state of sincerity and simplicity of a devoted servant.

A large portion of the non-Jewish world worships an individual Jew, whom it calls "the son of God." The non-

Jewish world must come to recognize that *all* Jews are sons of God. *Bnei Noach* must strive to help the Jews fulfill their purpose on earth. Not by worshiping them as one worships God, but by realizing that complete and sincere service of God entails the continual readiness to serve and come to the aid of His people Israel in bringing redemption to the world. Only then will the true Messiah be revealed.

Foundation: Experiencing Divine Providence

"God's seal is truth,"[64] state the sages. Normally we understand truth as being the opposite of falsehood—an epistemological concept. Yet, in Hebrew there is another meaning to the word "truth": verification, or fulfillment.[65] God's "seal of truth" is manifest in the soul's drive to fulfill itself—the inner experience of the *sefirah* of foundation. God's seal of truth represents the conclusion of the emotive powers of the soul. Truth in this context is the experience of the soul's fundamental drive to pursue creativity—the drive to realize latent potential and make our deepest promises, to ourselves and others, come true.

The archetypal soul of foundation in the Torah is Joseph, the son of Jacob. Foundation is the extension of beauty, Jacob's *sefirah*, as alluded to in the verse: "These are the generations of Jacob, Joseph...."[66] Foundation is the *sefirah* identified with the *tzadik*, the holy individual who stands as the firm foundation of his generation.[67]

The first individual whom the Torah calls a *tzadik* is Noah. He alone fulfilled the potential of his generation, which perished in the Flood. It is to him that God granted, for the first time since the creation of Adam, permission to eat the meat of animals and at the same time forbade him (and all his offspring) from eating limbs amputated from live animals.[68] This prohibition protects the power of foundation and its inner dimension—truth.

Forbidden food numbs the innate sensitivity of the soul to perceive Divine Providence in all aspects of life. The Torah forbids *Bnei Yisrael* from consuming many types of food. But, more than any of the foods that are forbidden to Jews, the impulsive and animalistic act of tearing flesh from a living animal and eating it—the one form of sustenance forbidden to *Bnei Noach*—numbs the spiritual sensitivity of the soul.

Impulsivity is the behavior antithetical to that of the true *tzadik*. A *tzadik* is by definition a giver[69]—he receives only for the purpose of giving.[70] In order to give properly, the *tzadik* must possess both the wisdom to know to whom to give and when,[71] and consummate self-control to wait for the proper moment to give to the worthy cause and to refrain from giving to unworthy causes.[72] When a *tzadik* eats he is giving his body nourishment,[73] knowing that only a healthy body can serve as a vessel for the soul to complete its mission on earth.[74] Both the *tzadik*'s wisdom and his power of self-control are products of his keen sensitivity to Divine Providence.[75]

As we saw above (in regard to the *sefirah* of victory), total confidence in God results in a rectified state of self-confidence. Likewise, a keen sense of Divine Providence over each and every one of God's creations results in the ability to realize our inner potential and fulfill our goals in life. The more we realize that it is only by God's Providence over us that we succeed in life's missions, the more we gain access to the God-given power to actualize our potential and fulfill our goals.

We may now define the sixth principle of Divine meditation and service for *Bnei Noach*: recognizing Divine Providence at work in the world.

Like an artist who signs his name on a painting, God signs every element of reality with His attribute of truth. This Divine signature is the eternal impression of God's Presence and His Divine Providence in reality. Truly, He is omnipresent and omniscient.[76]

Guiding a thread through our discussion of the *sefirot* of loving-kindness, beauty, and foundation we may say that: God creates the world with love; He works miracles with mercy; and He makes His Presence and His Providence known to creation with truth.[77]

We are taught that Divine Providence watches over and determines the immediate and long-term fate of even the tiniest, inanimate element of creation, and most certainly that of living beings.[78] It is Divine Providence that gauges and regulates the pulse of life within every living being, endowing life with continuity.

There are two levels of awareness with regard to Divine Providence. One is the recognition of God's concern for the fate of each of His creations. The second is the infinitely greater recognition of how the individual fate of each and every creature advances God's universal purpose.[79] Every event in the cosmos—from the microcosm to the macrocosm— is intricately intertwined with every other. We see this in nature in the delicate balance of ecosystems. All of creation contributes to the fulfillment of God's ultimate purpose: "to make Him a dwelling place below."[80]

It is only when this physical world that we live in—the lowest level of reality—recognizes the transcendent light that permeates the universe, and thus becomes a part of that light, that God's Presence can come to dwell among us.[81] The Psalms[82] affirm that, "Your judgments reach into the abyss; man and animal shall You save, O' GOD."[83]

Kingdom: Making a Home for God on Earth

Humility, the inner experience of kingdom, does not imply the negation of self, but rather the experience of oneself as existentially distant from God. Humility, as a positive spiritual state, is the product of realizing that I take up a lot of space and leave little room for God, that it is my own pride and sense of self that keeps God distant from revealing Himself in His world. The Torah teaches that God prefers the humble individual who forever questions and doubts his nearness to God than the one that feels that he has already succeeded in bringing God into His world. Humility is thus the constant source for the soul's motivation to return to God, to grow near to Him, and to make a home for the Almighty on earth.[84]

As explained in the previous chapter, the last of the seven Laws of *Bnei Noach* prescribes the establishment of a legal system to enforce the other laws and corresponds to the *sefirah* of kingdom and to its inner experience: humility before God. Thus, the seventh and final principle of Divine meditation and service for *Bnei Noach* is creating a kingdom for God on earth. Let us further explore this correspondence.

The responsibility to establish a legal system falls on the community, on society at large, rather than on each particular individual. Of course, each of us must do our utmost, utilizing all of the resources we have within our sphere of influence, to ensure that the community we live in establishes courts of justice. Humans are by nature social and political beings. We should give first priority to rectify our society, and a rectified society begins with a just legal system.

Our society is our extended home, a place in which we want to feel comfortable. When we live in accordance with God's Will (which of course is for our own ultimate good) and care for the welfare of our society by establishing courts of justice, our world becomes God's home—a place where He can feel comfortable, so to speak.

Most obviously, a legal system sharpens the sense of responsibility that each member of the society has for his deeds. Ideally, the social call for justice serves to inspire every member of the community to better his deeds and to live up to his potential. Social responsibility is thus the beginning of the conscious endeavor to return to God, to make Him a home on earth.

Clearly, in order to establish a legal system to enforce the other laws and to inform all people of the myriad details of each of their Laws, *Bnei Noach* must be willing to learn from the sages of *Bnei Yisrael* the intricacies of the Torah that pertain to the establishment of a rectified world order.[85] In this respect *Bnei Yisrael* and *Bnei Noach* must take on the archetypical roles of male and female, or giver and receiver, respectively.

Let us say a few words about the nature of the male and female principles in reality. All stages of the creative process— the evolution of worlds one from another, the interaction between them, and their ultimate unification—depend upon the dynamic of male and female energies which manifest as giving and receiving. The will to give and the will to receive are two fundamental cosmic forces. The will to give is portrayed in Kabbalah as a convex projection. The will to receive is portrayed as a concave receptacle.[86]

The relationship of *Bnei Yisrael* (a nation of priests who deliver God's word) to *Bnei Noach* follows this model. *Bnei Yisrael* are the givers of God's teachings to *Bnei Noach*, the receivers.

To realize that one is but an empty vessel waiting to receive Divine sustenance is to experience true humility, which translates into a recognition of our total dependence on the benevolence of God. The Creator's ultimate desire in creating the world is that our state of reality (which is the lowest of all) become His dwelling place—a home in which His absolute essence may be revealed. In the soul, it is the experience and state of humility that creates the concave receptacle, the dwelling place, for the Almighty.[87] It is the alluring vacuum of the empty vessel (the receiver) that pulls and draws down into itself the projection of the giver. The image of an empty vessel, i.e., of a person willing and eager to hear the teachings of the Torah, reminds the Torah sage of the origin of the receiver, the feminine principle, which in Kabbalah is described as preceding the origin of the giver, the masculine principle.[88] He then yearns to infuse the empty vessel with all that he can.

To understand the relationship of Jew and non-Jew more fully, a relationship which brings each to experience humility (the inner experience of kingdom) in face of the other, let us first note that the origin of non-Jewish souls is in the primordial World of Chaos (*tohu*) that preceded the World of Rectification (*tikun*), the origin of Jewish souls. In the World of Chaos the lights were great (infinitely more brilliant than the lights that shine, initially, in the World of Rectification) but the vessels were small and immature, unable to contain the great lights. And so, the vessels broke and fell into the realm of the lower worlds, where self-consciousness, feeling separate from

God, reigns. The vessels of the World of Rectification, on the other hand, are well-developed, and capable of holding their lights (though greatly diminished, initially, in relation to the lights of the World of Chaos). For this reason human life (which in general is related to the World of Rectification) is sustained by food from the animal and vegetable kingdoms, which contain the fallen sparks and vessels of the primordial World of Chaos. And for this very reason, a Jew realizes that there is something more primal in the being of the non-Jew than in his own.

Nonetheless, we are taught in Kabbalah and Chassidut that the ultimate source of the World of Rectification precedes, in the mind of God, the World of Chaos, for rectification is the state of reality that God initially desired in creation. And so it is right for both Jew and non-Jew to possess a certain state of humility each in the face of the other. The humility of the Jew before the non-Jew should be made conscious only when facing a non-Jew who has chosen to become a righteous gentile, an authentic *Ben Noach*.

Righteous non-Jewish souls long to ascend from a limited physical perspective to a more mature Divine perspective on reality—to take hold, as it were, of God's "signature," as represented by Israel, "God's firstborn son."[89] It is the receiver who arouses the will of the giver to come forth. When the giver and the receiver connect, the Divine Presence descends to illuminate lower reality.

In our present context, the relationship of the Jewish people to the non-Jewish world, the Torah limits the giver-receiver association to a purely spiritual and intellectual relationship of teacher to student. In order for this relationship to be productive, both teacher and student must experience humility—how at present each, alone, is far from God—and be motivated by humility to enter the relationship for the sake of making God a dwelling place on earth.

Chassidut teaches that a teacher-student relationship is similar in many ways to the relationship of husband and wife. We thus conclude with the thought that the rectified relationship of Jew and non-Jew is a partnership of humility—almost like the partnership of marriage.[90] The wife, serving as a devoted helpmate, thereby expresses her dependence on her husband, while the husband, sensing that the origin of his wife's soul precedes that of his own, displays his own dependence on his wife. God Himself is the "third partner"[91] of every marriage; it is by His power that the marriage becomes consummate and fruitful.

Of course, it goes without saying that intermarriage between Jew and non-Jew is strictly prohibited (even if the non-Jew is a righteous gentile, a *ger toshav*, who, in the Messianic era is permitted to live in the Land of Israel). Only with full conversion to Judaism does marriage with a Jew become permissible (with the exception of a Cohen, one who is a descendant of Aaron the High Priest, who is forbidden to marry a convert). The analogy of marriage between the Jewish people and the nations, in Messianic times, presented here, is intended only to portray the ideal state of working together towards the common goal of making our earth a dwelling place for the Creator.

Notes:

1. For a definition of contemplative Kabbalah, see *What You Need to Know About Kabbalah*, pp. 29ff.

2. For a more complete discussion of this see *What You Need to Know About Kabbalah*, chapter 7. See also Alter Rebbe's *Torah Or* 13c-14a for this as well as our Hebrew volume *Sod Hashem Liyerei'av*, chapter 1.

3. In Judaism, the love between a man and a woman mirrors the love between God and Israel, as depicted most eloquently in the Song of Songs.

4. *Tanya, Sha'ar Hayichud Veha'emunah*, ch. 2.

5. Psalms 89:3.

6. Genesis 2:4.

7. The very fact that this is the grammatical form of the word for "creation" in the first verse of the second account of creation in the Torah alludes to the fact that the world was not only created once, in the remote past, but is continuously being re-created through the channel of the soul-root of Abraham, the Divine attribute of love. This is similar to the beginning of *Tanya*, the classic text of Chassidut, where the natural/animal soul is described in the first chapter and the Divine soul of Israel— defined as the second soul—is discussed only in the second chapter.

8. *Zohar* I, 230b, and elsewhere.

9. Genesis 12:5.

10. See *Rashi* to Genesis 12:11.

11. These wounds are a result of the breaking of the vessels in the primordial World of Chaos, described in length in the writings of the Arizal.

12. The numerical value of Abraham (אַבְרָהָם) is 248, the number of limbs in the human body (Mishnah *Ohalot* 1:8), corresponding to the number of positive commandments in the Torah (*Makot* 23b). When all of the limbs are complete, one is consummately healthy.

13. Genesis 20:17.

14. Ibid. 31:42.

15. Ibid. 27:40. Esau personifies degenerate fear, just as Ishmael, Abraham's son, personifies degenerate love, which, in addition to inciting sexual violations, misdirects one to love oneself instead of others, ultimately leading to extreme vigilance for one's imagined honor.

16. *Berachot* 33b, and elsewhere. The numerical value of the idiom "the fear of Heaven" (יְרְאַת שָׁמַיִם) is 1001, alluding to the sages' saying that all—1000—is in the hands of Heaven, except for 1—the fear of Heaven.

A similar idea is expressed by the sages (*Chagigah* 9b) regarding the difference between reviewing one's studies 100 times and reviewing them 101 times (see also *Tanya*, chapter 15). The 101st time counts more than all of the 100, and so the fear of Heaven counts more, for God the Creator of the universe, than the entire universe and all that exists and happens in it. All was created for man possessing free choice to fear God, and only by choosing correctly does the ultimate purpose of all of creation become fulfilled, i.e., creating a dwelling place for the Almighty.

There is an additional saying of the sages that begins with the phrase, "All is in the hands of Heaven except for...": "All is in the hands of Heaven except for fevers and colds" (*Ketubot* 30a). The similarity of these two sayings indicates that just as it is up to the free will of man to guard his physical health (so as not to catch a cold), so it is up to his free will to guard his spiritual health by fearing God and refraining to go against His will. The most basic fear of man is the fear of disease and its consequence—death. There is no better way to guard one's health—and free oneself from the psychological enslavement to the fear of disease—than to fear Heaven (and no other).

In Maimonides' Code of Law, the *Mishneh Torah*, there are exactly 1000 chapters. One of the chapters (*Hilchot De'ot* 4) is devoted to guarding one's physical health (for the sake of being able to serve God to the utmost). And so we may conclude that from the perspective of the Torah, physical health is 1 out of 1000, meaning that a person should devote 1/10th of one percent of his spiritual effort to his physical health. But, fear of God, which is equal to 1001, demands 1/10th of one percent more than all of one's natural spiritual capacity. By exerting and stretching our spiritual abilities in order to attain fear and awe of God, we merit that our pursuit of physical health also be successful, with minimal effort.

17. Psalms 100:2.

18. Ibid. 2:11. In Hebrew, the two words, "in joy" (בְּשִׂמְחָה) and "in fear/awe" (בְּיִרְאָה) possess identical vocalization (vowel) signs: *shva, chirik, shva, kamatz*. The final words of the second phrases of both verses, "with song" (בִּרְנָנָה) and "with trembling" (בִּרְעָדָה), also possess identical vocalization signs: *chirik, shva, kamatz, kamatz*. Thus, the two verses rhyme. In Kabbalah, this means that the two forms of spiritual service expressed in the two verses possess a common source in the super-conscious pleasure of the soul—the origin of song and poetry. The realization that conscious experience of joy derives from super-conscious pleasure is more obvious than the realization that conscious experience of fear/awe derives from the same super-conscious source of pleasure (as emphasized in the continuation: "Serve God with fear/awe and be joyful whilst trembling").

The key to understanding this apparent paradox lies in the phrase common to the two verses: "Serve God." For the essence of the soul, nothing is more pleasurable than serving God, the infinite source of all life (and pleasure), each individual in his own way. For the Jew this means serving God primarily with joy, while for the non-Jew this means serving God primarily with fear/awe. In the terminology of Kabbalah, these two manners of serving God derive ultimately from the front and the back (or the male side and the female side) of the super-conscious pleasure principle, known in Kabbalistic terminology as *Atik Yomin*—the Ancient of Days.

19. It is important to realize that the ladder of faith can be climbed by every human being; anyone whose soul moves him or her to do so can become a Jew through proper conversion.

20. Fear of punishment, at its root, is fear of death or fear of murder. Psychologically, this relates to the lion syndrome, described at length in *Body, Mind, and Soul*, p. 109ff., the phobia that corresponds to an imbalance in the *sefirah* of might.

21. As referred to in Psalms 2:11 quoted above.

22. Ultimately, a Jew turns to God in love, the love of a son for his father. A non-Jew first turns to God in fear, the fear of a servant of his master. Nonetheless, it is the fear in the Jewish soul that elevates the fear of the non-Jew to a state of awe and love as well.

23. See *Rashi ad. loc.*

24. According to Chassidic lore, even hell, the ultimate object of the fear of punishment, has burnt itself up completely. Hell has been replaced by what was previously paradise, and the old paradise has been replaced by a totally new one.

25. Maimonides, *Hilchot Yesodei Hatorah* 2:2.

26. *Avodah Zarah* 3b. Rosh Hashanah, the first day of the new year, is the day that God judges all of His creations. The Almighty commanded the Jewish people to blow the *shofar* (a ram's horn) on this day in order to arouse Him, as it were, to rise from the throne of severe judgment and to sit on His throne of mercy. In Hebrew, the root of the word *shofar* is one of the synonyms for "beauty" (See *The Art of Education*, Supplementary Essay F, pp. 246ff.). This clearly relates the arousal to judge mercifully, with empathy for the other, to the *sefirah* of beauty and its inner dimension, mercy.

27. Genesis 43:14. Rabbi Nachman of Breslov notes (*Likutei Moharan* II, 62) that the initials of this phrase in Hebrew (אֵל שַׁדַּי יִתֵּן לָכֶם רַחֲמִים) spell Jacob's God-given name, Israel (יִשְׂרָאֵל), implying that Jacob's Divine essence is mercy.

28. *Tanya, Sha'ar Hayichud Veha'emunah*, chapter 5.

29. "A thief, when about to steal, beseeches God for help" (*Ein Ya'akov* to *Berachot* 63b). This is a classic example of this world being a world of dreams (Psalms 126:1). In a dream, opposites exist simultaneously (*Torah Or* 28c). In Hebrew, the word for

"dream," *chalom*, is cognate to the name of the vowel sign, *cholem*, which corresponds in Kabbalah to the *sefirah* of beauty. Jacob's dream, the ladder that connects heaven and earth, is the archetypal dream of the Torah, and indeed Jacob is the archetypal soul of the *sefirah* of beauty. In the *Zohar* (I, 266b) we find that Jacob's ladder symbolizes the spiritual service of prayer, the service of the heart (*Ta'anit* 2a), in general, and of the *sefirah* of beauty, in particular, as will be explained.

30. This derived from the fact that throughout the first account of creation (Genesis 1:1 – 2:3), the only Name of God used is the Name *Elokim*, the Name that connotes God's attribute of (severe) judgment. But the first verse of the second account of creation (Genesis 2:4) introduces God's essential Name, *Havayah*, the Name that connotes God's attribute of mercy. In this verse the two Names—*Havayah Elokim*—appear together, with *Havayah* preceding *Elokim*. From this we learn that God initially considered creating the world with (severe) judgment, i.e., creating a world in which each individual is judged exactly in accordance with the merit of his deeds and intentions. But He saw, as it were, that such an "ideal" world—where the attribute of (severe) judgment would motivate all to be consummately righteous—could not persevere. And so He created the world with His attribute of mercy together with, and before, His attribute of (severe) judgment, in order to insure that His judgment be directed by His mercy.

31. Psalms 145:9.

32. From the fact that God created nature, with its fixed laws, we learn that God loves nature. But sometimes His love and compassion for a certain individual or people supercedes His attachment to nature and its laws, and He works miracles. In working miracles, He reveals that He is the Creator of nature and that nature is in His hands to alter at His will.

33. The fundamental law of Divine judgment is referred to as the law of "measure for measure" (*Sanhedrin* 90a). This reflects the second emotive force.

34. According to a Chassidic adage, "After a fire one becomes rich." This means that God's attribute of (severe) judgment is followed by His attribute of mercy and compassion.

35. Rabbi Shneur Zalman explains (*Tanya, Sha'ar Hayichud Veha'emunah,* chapter 5) that the Divine attribute of mercy (which God placed before His attribute of severe judgment in the creation of the universe) is "the revelation of Divinity by *tzadikim* [consummately righteous individuals] and the signs and wonders of the Torah [i.e., the miracles related in the Torah]." In Kabbalah, God's Name of mercy, *Havayah,* the Torah, and miracles (wrought by God for the sake of His people Israel) all relate to the *sefirah* of beauty. "The revelation of Divinity by *tzadikim*" alludes, in particular, to the *sefirah* of foundation which is the extension of the *sefirah* of beauty—"The *tzadik* is the foundation of the world" (Proverbs 10:25). This will become clear in the meditation relating to the *sefirah* of foundation where the full manifestation of Divine Providence becomes revealed through the means of the *tzadik* of the generation.

36. *Berachot* 7a, and elsewhere.

37. *Shabbat* 151b.

38. Israel is the name that God gave to Jacob, the third patriarch, who corresponds, in Kabbalah, to the *sefirah* of beauty. For this reason, we find in the Bible the idiom "the beauty of Israel" (Lamentations 2:1). The Jewish people descend from the children of Jacob, whose "bed was unblemished" (*Midrash Vayikra Rabah* 36:5; see *Rashi* to Genesis 28:21), meaning that all of his children inherited holy souls of Israel, not like Abraham, the first patriarch (who corresponds to the *sefirah* of loving-kindness), who gave birth to Ishmael, and not like Isaac, the second patriarch (who corresponds to the *sefirah* of might), who gave birth to Esau. See also above note 27.

39. From the prayers of Rosh Hashanah. The final letters of the four words of this phrase (בַּקֵּשׁ רַחֲמִים כְּעָנִי בַּפֶּתַח) permute to spell Messiah (מָשִׁיחַ). The numerical value of the words, "a poor man at the doorstep" (עָנִי בַּפֶּתַח), 620, equals the numerical value of

"crown" (כֶּתֶר). The *sefirah* of beauty is the central point of the middle axis of the Tree of Life, and is referred to as the middle pillar that ascends to the crown and descends to kingdom. The "poor man at the doorstep" is the initial state of consciousness of kingdom, who by humbly beseeching God to shower upon him His infinite mercy (the inner experience of beauty) ascends to receive the super-conscious crown by which the poor man transforms into a king.

40. In the terminology of the sages, all forms of idolatry are referred to as "serving stars and constellations [i.e., the signs of the zodiac]." According to this belief-system, the destiny of every soul on earth is foretold by the stars at the moment of one's birth. There is no room for real change or spiritual metamorphosis.

41. See Maimonides, *Hilchot Isurei Bi'ah* 14:7-8 and *Hilchot Melachim* 8:10.

42. Leviticus 19:34 and Deuteronomy 10:19.

43. The concluding words of the Torah are "which Moses did before the eyes of all Israel," which according to Chassidic tradition alludes to the essential bond of the two souls—Moses and Israel Ba'al Shem Tov.

44. Of King David, the archetypal soul of the *sefirah* of kingdom, and even more so of his descendant, the Messiah son of David (who, the sages connote as "a miscarriage," *Yalkut Shimoni Bereisheet* 41), it is said that he experienced himself as continuously dying (like a miscarried fetus) and requiring God's mercy to sustain his life at every moment. This experience is slightly different from the one described here (the experience of the *sefirah* of victory). Here one experiences being created altogether anew, whereas the experience of David is one of continual death and coming back to life.

45. Victory is the last *sefirah* on the right axis of the Tree of Life. The first *sefirah* on the right axis is wisdom. Of wisdom it is said, "and wisdom shall be found from naught" (Job 28:12), from which we learn that the power of creation ex-nihilo is associated

in particular with the *sefirah* of wisdom. Those greatest of souls, that experience spiritual metamorphosis continuously, merit Divine wisdom—for the initial point on the right axis, wisdom, becomes fully reflected and manifest in the final point, victory— the power to re-create even in the external realm of this world.

46. Moses decreed that God create a mouth for the earth. The power of the *tzadik* (the consummately righteous individual) to decree things that the Almighty subsequently performs is one of the Nine Principles of Faith of the inner teachings of the Torah, which complement the Thirteen Principles of Faith compiled by Maimondes. This particular principle corresponds to the *sefirah* of victory, as explained in the Hebrew volume *Emunah Ve'muda'oot*.

47. Numbers 16:30.

48. See *Ta'anit* 25a a similar story regarding Rabbi Chaninah ben Dosa.

49. Immersion in purifying waters is itself a process of spiritual metamorphosis. Covered by the waters, one returns to a state of nothingness, to be reborn as a new something when resurfacing.

50. The greatest feat (miracle) that a Chassidic master can perform is turning a "log" into a human being, i.e., transforming the character of a person without the initial makings of an upright individual into one.

51. *Tanya*, chapter 1.

52. *Onkelos* (Aramaic translation to the Torah) on Deuteronomy 18:13.

53. Genesis 25:27. In the Passover *Hagadah* the simpleton son is called a *tam*.

54. These three different manifestations of sincerity correspond to the three definitions of sincerity given in the beginning of Rabbi Dov Ber Schneersohn's *Derech Chaim*.

55. Exodus 4:22. See also above p. 49 n. 29.

56. *Tanya*, chapter 2; based on Job 31:2.

57. *Kidushin* 36a. But, Rabbi Me'ir says that regardless of their status the Jewish people are considered God's sons, meaning that the essence of being a son always remains. The fact that the greatest of *tzadikim*, like Moses, are called "God's servant" (Deuteronomy 34:5) constitutes a higher level known as "a son who has become a servant," a concept explained in length in the fifth Lubavitcher Rebbe's *Sefer Hama'amarim 5666*.

58. Chassidut explains that even a *tzadik* may fall from his spiritual level. The purpose of such a fall is that the *tzadik* have the opportunity to meet lower souls "on their turf" and with merely his presence, strengthen them and inspire them to rise higher. The same is true of the Jewish people as a whole. Their fall is designed so that they can strengthen and inspire the nations of the world to reach higher and embrace God and His Torah truthfully. Of course, all such falls can only be considered positive as long as they do not overstep the boundaries of holiness. For the individual *tzadik* this translates into falling into the state of an intermediary (a *beinoni*, in the *Tanya*). For the Jewish people it means falling from serving God as a son to serving Him as a servant, that is without an inner sense of joy. A servant, though he has no inner joy in performing the commandments themselves, nonetheless, continues to perform them.

59. III, 53b.

60. By demonstrating his own love for God, Aaron aroused the individual Jew's love for God by example. The righteous gentile who has committed to God, His Torah, and His people can arouse the individual Jew's love for God in a similar manner by providing a challenge: if a non-Jew can love God so much, how much more so should a Jew, a member of God's betrothed people, be able to love God.

61. According to the *Zohar* (III, 103a), Eliezer the servant of Abraham was no other than Canaan, the son of Cham the son of Noah, who was cursed by his grandfather to be a slave to his brothers (Genesis 9:25). According to Kabbalah, this means that Eliezer

was a reincarnation of Canaan and returned to this world to rectify, in part, the transgression of Canaan (who was responsible for his father's defiling Noah, while drunken and naked in his tent). In the merit of his devoted service of Abraham, and in particular his dedication to find the Divinely ordained wife for Isaac, he merited to undergo spiritual metamorphosis, and existentially transform from one who is "cursed" to one that is "blessed" (see *Zohar* ibid.).

Significantly, Eliezer the servant of Abraham continued to reincarnate in Eliezer the son of Moses and, after many more stops along the way, in Eliezer the father of the Ba'al Shem Tov. Once more (as before, in relation to the transformation process associated with the *sefirah* of victory), the figures of Moses and the Ba'al Shem Tov appear (here, in virtue of their son/father— Eliezer) as the pillars of inspiration for the righteous gentile wishing to come closer to God and His people Israel and convert to the status of a *ger toshav*—a righteous gentile who is permitted to dwell in the Land of Israel.

62. Genesis 12:3. The original blessing to mankind was "You shall be fruitful and multiply" (Genesis 1:22). There can be no greater blessing for Abraham than to find the Divinely ordained wife for his only son (from Sarah), Isaac, of whom God had promised him "for in Isaac will your seed be called" (Ibid. 21:12). And so, in virtue of Eliezer's dedication to find Rebecca for Isaac, he merited to be transformed into a "blessed" individual.

63. Genesis 24:34.

64. *Yoma* 69b, and elsewhere.

65. In Kabbalah, epistemological truth is related to the intellect, the *sefirot* of wisdom and understanding.

66. Genesis 37:2. Foundation lies directly underneath beauty on the middle axis of the Tree of Life (which possesses the power to stabilize the otherwise unstable extremities of right and left, the essence of *tikun*, rectification), making Jacob's relationship with his son, Joseph, unique. Beauty (Jacob) does not lie directly

underneath might (Isaac), situated on the left axis, nor does might (Isaac) lie underneath loving-kindness (Abraham), situated on the right axis. Both Abraham, the right, and Isaac, the left, lived before the appearance of the stabilizing middle, Jacob. For this reason, both Abraham and Isaac gave birth to a degenerate offspring, while Jacob's offspring (generated by the soul root of Joseph, the manifestation of mercy as truth, as explained in Chassidut) were all holy and in the idiom of the sages: "His bed was unblemished," i.e., none of his offspring deviated from his path (see note 38 above).

67. "And the *tzadik* is the foundation of the world" (Proverbs 10:25).

68. As noted above, there are two opinions as to who—Adam, or Noah—was given the prohibition of eating the flesh of a live animal.

69. A *tzadik* is defined as one who gives *tzedakah*, charity (both words are from the same root).

70. The *sefirah* of foundation, the ninth of the ten *sefirot*, receives from the *sefirot* above it in order to channel, in a well-measured and regulated manner, the influx of Divine energy into the *sefirah* of kingdom.

71. In Kabbalah, the foundation contained within the *sefirah* of wisdom, extends until it enters the *sefirah* of foundation proper, thereby providing the *tzadik* the wisdom necessary for giving properly.

72. See *The Art of Education*, pp. 130-4. The power of self-control comes to the *tzadik*, the *sefirah* of foundation, from the *sefirah* of might. In the idiom of Kabbalah, foundation, though located on the middle axis of the *sefirot*, tends to the left, in order to receive the power of self-control from might.

In the Torah, the power of self-control is attributed to the archetypal figure of the true *tzadik*, Joseph. Joseph was able to subdue his sexual arousal (Genesis 43:31).

73. "The *tzadik* eats to sustain himself" (Proverbs 13:25)—neither more nor less. As noted in the *Tanya* (chapter 29), the *tzadik* sees

it as a holy duty to sustain his body. When Hillel the Elder would go to eat he would say that he was going to perform an act of kindness with the poor one—i.e., with his body.

74. "That the body be healthy and wholesome is part of Divine service, for a person cannot know or understand anything of what there is to know about the Divine if the body is sick..." (Maimonides, *Hilchot De'ot* 4:1).

75. Which itself becomes keener and keener as his body becomes more and more refined by eating with only the purpose of giving in mind.

76. The sages teach that "one who gives bread to a child should inform the child's mother" (*Shabbat* 10b). In Kabbalah and Chassidut we learn that both child and mother are but two facets of one psyche. The child refers to the emotive attributes of the heart, while the mother refers to the understanding of the soul, or more generally, to the soul's consciousness.

Everything that God created in the world is for us, i.e., bread for the child (for we are identified with the figure denoted in Kabbalah as "the Small Countenance," *Zeir Anpin*, constructed, primarily from the six *sefirot* that correspond to the six emotive attributes of the heart, from loving-kindness to foundation). As an artist, God signs His Name on every one of His creations, i.e., informs the mother of the gift's origin.

Foundation is the sixth of the emotive powers, the conclusion of the child's body. Foundation also represents the final stage of the child's physical and psychological development (maturity, in essence a state of mind, is reflected in the functioning of the body's procreative organ, which corresponds to the *sefirah* of foundation). Here, upon reaching the final stage of giving the gift to the child—representing the final, culminating stage in the creation of reality—the Giver, God, signs His signature of truth on His handiwork, telling us where it came from. And so we learn that foundation reaches all the way up to understanding. In Kabbalah, this explains the teaching of the sages that Joseph (foundation) reminded Jacob (the Small Countenance) of his mother Rachel (who after passing away ascended from kingdom to understanding).

77. The ability to recognize continual re-creation is the principle of Divine meditation and service that comes from the *sefirah* of loving-kindness. The recognition that God works miracles (which arouses us to pray to God) relates to the *sefirah* of beauty. The recognition of God's continual Providence over each and every one of His creations relates to the *sefirah* of foundation. Just as re-creation is continual, so is God's Providence over all. Moreover, Divine Providence is the driving force of re-creation (as explained in a letter on Divine Providence from the Lubavitcher Rebbe, see the Lubavitcher Rebbe's *Igrot Kodesh*, v. 1, epistle 94; see also *Hayom Yom* for the 29th of Sivan). And so, "the end [of the six *sefirot* from loving-kindness to foundation, which correspond to the six days of creation] is embedded in the beginning [of the six *sefirot*]" (*Sefer Yetzirah* 1:7).

Miracles, which supersede the laws of nature, appear to be few and far-between. But, indeed miracles that are invisible to us are always happening. The more sensitive one becomes to Divine Providence as the directive force in the continual re-creation of nature with its fixed laws, the more one becomes capable of seeing actual, supernatural miracles occur in one's life and in the world surrounding him.

The average numerical value of loving-kindness (חֶסֶד, 72), beauty (תִּפְאֶרֶת, 1081), and foundation (יְסוֹד, 80) is 411, also the numerical value of the idiom "something from nothing," or ex-nihilo (יֵשׁ מֵאַיִן). The very fact that God continually creates something from nothing relates to the first principle of loving-kindness— continual re-creation. The inner dynamic of the process by which God creates something from nothing relates to the third principle of foundation—Divine Providence. The more one is able to connect to the nothing from which the something is created, the more one becomes sensitive to the second principle of beauty— miracles.

78. The Talmud relates (*Chulin* 63a) that when observing even the smallest creatures the sages would recite the verse: "Your [God's] righteousness is like the mighty mountains, Your judgments reach into the abyss. Man and animal shall You save, O' GOD" (Psalms 36:7), for this verse describes God's Providence over all creatures.

79. *Hayom Yom* for the 28th of *Cheshvan*. The first level is God overseeing the world from the perspective of the World of Emanation (where all is conscious of God alone). The second is God overseeing the world from the perspective of Primordial Man, *Adam Kadmon* (where all of creation is perceived simultaneously, before even the consciousness of God alone has come into being). From the perspective of the World of Creation (where the independent, self-consciousness of created beings becomes a possibility), Divine Providence over nature is general and not detailed, i.e., His Providence is over species (the real entities of the World of Formation) but not over individuals (the real entities of the World of Action). This understanding of Divine Providence was put forth by the Jewish philosophers, most notably Maimonides, whose philosophical speculations and conjectures reached the conscious awareness of the World of Creation (two worlds above our own), as explained elsewhere.

80. *Midrash Tanchuma Naso* 16.

81. This ultimate consciousness of Divine Providence is displayed by the *tzadik*, the righteous one of Israel. In each generation there is one *tzadik* who, by virtue of his completely rectified state of consciousness, is "the foundation of the world." The closer one is to the *tzadik* of the generation, the greater one's level of consciousness is with regard to Divine Providence, especially that which is revealed in one's own life. With regard to non-Jewish souls without conscious connection to the *tzadik* (and Israel, in this context, can be seen as the *tzadik* of the world as a whole), the Divine Providence watching over them is hardly visible. In this state, that which they experience as Providence

reaches them only after passing through many intermediate spiritual levels.

82. 37:7.

83. This verse is understood by the sages as a reference to God's individual Providence over all of creation. In Kabbalah it is taught that salvation is brought to the world when animal connects to man. The terms "animal" and "man" are relative. Ultimately, "man" refers to the *tzadik*, "the foundation of the generation," whose consciousness is complete and true. All other souls (both Jewish and non-Jewish) are varying levels of "animal." Just as "man" directs the "animal," guiding it to fulfill and actualize its inner potential, so does the *tzadik*, the "man" of the generation, the one who is consummately conscious of God's purpose in creation, give a sense of direction in life to all those that connect to him. He is God's great emissary to the world. It is he who can reveal to every member of his generation his Divinely ordained task in life. Thus, here again we see that the thirst of the non-Jewish soul for salvation can only be quenched by clinging to the soul of Israel, in particular to "the *tzadik*, the foundation of the generation." The *tzadik* is in truth God's visible seal in creation, to whom the eyes of all creatures should be uplifted (in order to witness Divine Providence—the eyes of God—in all avenues of life).

84. The *sefirah* of kingdom corresponds to the final *hei* of God's essential Name, *Havayah*. Of the four letters of *Havayah*, the final *hei* is the only one that does not have another letter following it, symbolizing a lower level of Divine consciousness upon which it can rest or be supported. Therefore, only the final *hei* senses the absence of Divine consciousness below it. It feels itself far away from its true self and liable to fall into the abyss of loss of Divine consciousness (that only God exists in truth, there is no other besides Him). For this reason, of the *sefirah* of kingdom (which corresponds to the final *hei*) it is said, "Her feet descend unto [the realm of] death" (Proverbs 5:5). For a being in the World of Emanation, loss of Divine consciousness is equivalent to death.

Thus, kingdom, the final *hei*, clings the strongest to the letters above it, ever aware of its existential need to connect to the higher levels of Divine consciousness, for below it, the supporting hand of God is concealed (though, in truth, always present).

From the beginning of creation, and throughout the Bible, kingdom is referred to as "the earth," the bottom or ground level of creation. Of the earth it is said: "He [God] suspends the earth on nothing" (Job 26:7). The numerical value of this phrase (תֹּלֶה אֶרֶץ עַל בְּלִימָה), 913, exactly equals that of the very first word of the Torah, בְּרֵאשִׁית, "In the beginning." This teaches us that all of creation and all of history is for the sake of rectifying the *sefirah* of kingdom, so that the consciousness of the absolute Oneness of God and His Name should fill the earth—as stated by the prophet, "And GOD shall be king over the whole earth, on that day shall GOD be One and His Name One" (Zachariah 14:9). This itself is making for God a home on earth.

The *Zohar* (III, 122b) interprets the word *teshuvah* ("return to God") as "the *hei* shall return (to connect to the letters of God's Name above it)." Although there is a level of *teshuvah* referred to as "higher *teshuvah*" (*teshuvah ila'ah*), where the *Zohar's* interpretation of the *hei* returning to its source refers to the first *hei* of God's Name (returning to the consciousness of the *yud* and the tip of the *yud*), nonetheless, the primary meaning of the *Zohar's* interpretation of *teshuvah* is that the lower *hei*, the *hei* that is suspended on nothing, shall return to unite in perfect oneness with the previous letters of God's Name. The return from afar of the lower *hei*—"lower *teshuvah*" (*teshuvah tata'ah*)—is infinitely more intense than the return of the near (but longing to be nearer) higher *hei*. And so we learn in Chassidut that while there are blemishes of the soul that only the higher *teshuvah* can rectify, the essence of *teshuvah*, returning to God (from a state of spiritual exile), is the lower *teshuvah*, the *teshuvah* of kingdom, in true lowliness and humility, the inner experience of kingdom.

85. Several examples of non-obvious details of the laws that must be taught to *Bnei Noach* by a qualified Torah scholar will be brought in the next chapter.

86. The terms used in Kabbalah and Chassidut for "convex projection" and "concave receptacle" are *chotam bolet* and *chotam shokai'a*, literally, an "extroverted seal" and an "introverted seal." With these two seals God seals every aspect of creation. In particular, they correspond to the two *sefirot* of foundation and kingdom, or, more exactly, to the male foundation (symbolized, in the body, by the male procreative organ, the sign of the covenant) and to the female foundation, the foundation of kingdom (symbolized, in the body, by the womb).

87. A man's wife is called his dwelling place (*Yoma* 2a).

88. Chassidut explains that this idea is alluded to in the verse: "The Name of GOD is a strong tower, within it the *tzadik* runs and is elevated" (Proverbs 18:10). The *tzadik* who represents the masculine inclination to give is aroused to run, i.e., to extend himself and give, when he encounters the "strong tower," which is an appellation for the *sefirah* of kingdom, which represents the female inclination to humility. Elsewhere, Chassidut teaches that Moses was "more humble than any man on the face of the earth" (Numbers 12:3) including all non-Jews. In Chassidic teachings it is explained that this was because Moses honestly believed that if the Almighty had blessed some other individual with talents similar to his own, than that individual would have put them to even better use than he himself had.

89. This was the inner intent of Rachav of Jericho—who eventually converted and married Joshua—when she asked for a "true sign" (Joshua 2:12) from the spies. See also Arizal's *Likutei Torah* to Joshua 2.

90. See in length in *The Mystery of Marriage*, chapter 7.

91. "If a man and a woman merit, the Divine Presence dwells between them" (*Sotah* 17a).

Practical Applications of the Seven Laws of *Bnei Noach*

5

Serving the One God

Two trees grew in the Garden of Eden: the Tree of Knowledge of Good and Evil and the Tree of Life.[1] These two trees represent the two aspects of the soul—the physical aspect and the Divine aspect (as explained earlier). All the children of Adam and Eve have a natural affinity to the Tree of Knowledge. However, *Bnei Noach* (those who take upon themselves the seven Laws of *Bnei Noach* given by God to all humanity) also possess an affinity to the Tree of Life. The Torah is referred to as the Tree of Life:

> She [the Torah] is a tree of life to those who grasp her; and happy is every one who holds her fast...
> Her ways are ways of pleasantness, and all her paths are peace.[2]

To accept upon oneself the seven Laws of *Bnei Noach* is deceptively simple. After all, the laws themselves make sense, and it seems that all one needs is a desire to draw close to God and to uphold His universal instructions to all humanity. However, because the seven Laws of *Bnei Noach* are part and parcel of the Torah, to become a *Ben Noach*, one must first accept the truth of the Torah in its totality, including the truth of the oral traditions passed down from Moses through the generations.

Moreover, it should be absolutely clear that any non-Jew who seeks to become a righteous gentile committed to the seven Laws of *Bnei Noach* cannot define himself or herself as a member of any other religion. A righteous gentile is entirely devoted to the authenticity and truth of the Torah so that he or she can reveal the God of Israel to the entire world. This also means recognizing the Jewish people—*Bnei Yisrael*—as God's chosen people[3] and His nation of priests.[4]

In order to properly follow the seven Laws of *Bnei Noach*, those who choose to identify themselves as *Bnei Noach* must seek to learn from the Jews the deeper meaning of these commandments and their practical application as these were transmitted through the ages in the oral tradition of the Torah. In this way, they will be able to serve God as He desires.

While the seven Laws of *Bnei Noach* are clearly stated, their actual application requires detailed study.

For example, the law prohibiting theft is defined in the Torah as taking anything that belongs to another without his or her permission. While most people think of theft as breaking into a cash register and taking wads of money, the prohibition against stealing includes much more subtle actions. According to the Torah, borrowing a pen without permission is considered theft. If one works in an office and takes some paper home, that is also considered theft.

Similarly, the law prohibiting eating a limb off a live animal, has far reaching implications. Slaughter procedures in the Western world typically involve stunning the animal by firing a bullet into its brain, rendering it brain-dead, then proceeding to dismember the carcass while the animal's heart continues to beat. Eating meat from an animal killed in this manner violates this *Bnei Noach* commandment. It is clear from this that *Bnei Noach* would do well to eat meat slaughtered in the kosher manner.[5]

In addition, slander is considered to be a form of murder,[6] and the exact parameters of what is considered by the Torah to be adultery, idolatry, and blasphemy must be well defined for any individual *Ben Noach* or community of *Bnei Noach* as they appear in the complex totality of Torah law.

To properly keep their seven Laws, *Bnei Noach* must delve into these commandments with a qualified mentor who is a halachic authority.

Above all, to serve God, *Bnei Noach* must study His Torah. Parts of the Torah are relevant to non-Jews, and other parts are not. The parts of the Torah relevant to non-Jews are very deep, and would take more than a lifetime to study. These include the laws that apply to non-Jews in the revealed part of the Torah.

In addition, *Bnei Noach* should learn to meditate upon the mysteries of creation as revealed in the teachings of Kabbalah, the inner, hidden dimension of the Torah.[7] While in years past, only Jews who had extensive knowledge of the Talmud could comprehend the esoteric teachings of Kabbalah, today, thanks to the revelations brought down by the Ba'al Shem Tov, these teachings are accessible to all.[8] When Kabbalistic teachings are studied according to Chassidut, which explains everything in psychological terms, they are presented in a manner relevant to all truth seekers.[9] It is crucial however to study Kabbalah only from authentic sources.

The sages state that a non-Jew who seeks to know and connect to God from the depth of his heart may potentially reach levels of spirituality higher than those attained by the High Priest in the Holy Temple.[10] Certainly, a non-Jew who studies those Torah commandments which apply to him or her in depth and meditates upon the mysteries of creation as revealed in the teachings of Kabbalah that touch his or her soul can indeed attain great spiritual heights.

Ritual Observance for *Bnei Noach*

As explained earlier, the purpose of all humanity is *tikun olam* (the rectification of the world), which takes place when we spiritually liberate and retrieve the fragments or sparks of Divine light trapped within the material realm. The object is to ultimately reveal here, in our physical realm, the unity of God and to establish for Him a dwelling place on earth.

In all the ways that one serves God, one strives to accomplish this goal. The sages divided the service of the Almighty into three categories: study of the Torah, good deeds, and prayer. Each of these categories impacts the sparks of holiness trapped in the mundane in a different manner and together they work to elevate them:

- Through Torah study, one brings the awareness of the presence of the Divine spark hidden within reality into one's own consciousness.

- Through good deeds, one accomplishes the first stage of clarifying a spark—by pulling it out of its physical encrustation (called a *klipah*, meaning "shell," or "peel").

- Through prayer, one elevates that spark up to the highest spiritual realm.

Prayer

We have already discussed the importance of Torah study for *Bnei Noach*, and the importance of good deeds is self-evident, but are *Bnei Noach* obligated to pray?

In the introduction, we mentioned Rabbi Moshe Feinstein halachic ruling on this matter. Rabbi Feinstein argued that since the Torah tells us that the first individuals to establish rites of prayer were Abraham, Isaac, and Jacob (each of whom established one of the three daily prayers), therefore non-Jews, who by definition are not descended from the three Jewish patriarchs, have no obligation to pray on a regular, daily basis. But, just because there is no obligation, does not of course mean that non-Jews should not pray. On the contrary, prayer, for all peoples, is the deepest expression of one's belief in God and His Providence.

The prayers that are particularly pertinent to *Bnei Noach* are the Psalms, written by King David who is also called the sweet song-master of Israel. It is just as important to pray from the heart, in one's own words, with regard to every detail in one's personal life for which one seeks God's guiding hand and benevolence. It is good to pray to God that all of humanity will speedily come to recognize the truth of the Torah and will grow close to Him and to the observance of the *Bnei Noach* commandments.

Blessings

The Talmud relates that eating without blessing God for giving us the food is an act of theft.[11] The blessing to be recited by *Bnei Noach* may be phrased similarly to that which Jews recite: "Blessed are You, God, Master of the Universe, Who has created... [followed by the appropriate phrase according to the food being eaten]." After eating, *Bnei Noach* should bless God for His gift of life, health, and sustenance.

Shabbat

Bnei Noach are forbidden to observe the holy day of Shabbat as required of Jews (that is to abstain from the thirty-nine categories of work defined in the Torah). Instead, they may mark the day with additional Torah study and special prayers.

On Shabbat it is most appropriate to delve into those Torah teachings that address the coming of the true Messiah and his bringing peace and salvation to the entire world, for Shabbat is a day which heralds universal peace. *Bnei Noach* should pray that the visions of the prophets of Israel be fulfilled speedily in our days.

Holidays

Bnei Noach should be aware that each Jewish holiday envelopes within it a particular ability to heal the soul: Passover reinforces the soul's power to rectify our improper desire for physical wealth. *Shavuot* (the holiday of the giving of Torah at Mt. Sinai) reinforces the soul's power to rectify improper sexual desire. *Sukot* (the festival of booths) reinforces the soul's power to rectify the desire for gluttony and eating improper and unhealthy foods.[12]

By studying the nature of each of these faculties of the soul on its respective holiday, *Bnei Noach* can come to experience these holy days and integrate their energy into their lives. Under no circumstances may *Bnei Noach* invent new holidays, as this is tantamount to inventing a new religion, which is forbidden.[13]

In the Torah, the first day of the Hebrew month of *Tishrei*, Rosh Hashanah, ushers in the new year, and the tenth day of the month is prescribed as the holiest day of the year and a fast day; it is called Yom Kipur, the Day of Atonement. It is appropriate for non-Jews to adopt the spiritual significance of these days as days of repentance and prayer.

Fast Days

Fasting is a common spiritual custom and *Bnei Noach*, as people who are seeking an authentic spiritual life may benefit from it. In order to correctly incorporate fasting into one's spiritual life, it is important to know that the Rebbe Maharash, the fourth leader of the Chabad movement, explained that there are two types of fasts which are appropriate at all times for all people. These are:

- a fast of speech—to speak only that which is necessary and not to speak in order "to be heard."
- a fast of food—to eat only that which is necessary for the body's health, and not to eat just because something tastes good.

By applying these types of fasts in their lives, *Bnei Noach* can fast as often as they like and acquire great spiritual benefit from doing so.

Other Rituals

There are many other Jewish rituals that may be adopted by non-Jews after consulting with an Orthodox halachic authority who has agreed to serve as a legal and spiritual mentor for this purpose. For example, some *Bnei Noach* adopt the Jewish ritual manner of washing hands (*netilat yadayim*) before eating bread. Overall, cleanliness and care of the body and clothing are important in the service of God. Physical cleanliness leads to spiritual purity, as taught by the sages.[14]

Some *Bnei Noach* also choose to cover their heads as a reminder that God's Presence is above all. This is a positive thing to do, however it is not a good idea for *Bnei Noach* to choose a head covering that is identical to that commonly worn by Jews, as other people may mistake the non-Jew for a Jew. This may lead to confusion regarding the much more rigid conduct that the Torah requires of Jews. One way of making the head-covering distinct is by decorating it with the words "*Ben Noach*," or the like. (Likewise, Jews often decorate their skullcaps with their names or a phrase important to them.)

Life Rituals

Key events in life are auspicious times. These special moments, whether they be joyous (as in the birth of a child) or mournful (as at a funeral) open our hearts and the hearts of those around us in a special way. The opening of our heart and the hearts of our relatives and friends serves as the perfect opportunity for reaffirming our commitment to our beliefs and deepening them. Therefore, it is appropriate for *Bnei Noach* to seek the advice of a Jewish spiritual mentor on the proper form for celebrating or noting these special days. Here, we will address only a few key issues.

Marriage

It is most important for *Bnei Noach* to choose spouses who also desire to live in accordance with the seven Laws of *Bnei Noach*, and who consider loyalty in marriage a sacred duty. In the marriage ceremony of *Bnei Noach* it would be advisable to express this commitment to the sanctified nature of marriage publicly, and to make a covenant of loyalty to one another, and also with God. The covenant with God should express the intention of the couple to keep the seven Laws of *Bnei Noach*, and to help the Jewish people achieve their goal to bring redemption to the entire world.

The marriage ceremony is certainly a holy event, and we actually learn that God forgives all of the sins of the couple at this juncture in their lives.[15] A Rabbi can be present at the wedding. He can explain all of the above and bless the couple that they should merit to live a happy and fulfilling life together as they continue to grow close to God and His Torah.

Birth

Similarly, *Bnei Noach* can have a ceremony to celebrate the birth of a baby. The main part of this ceremony should include speaking before the guests about God's universal dictate to bear offspring.[16] Though this is not counted as one of the seven Laws, *Bnei Noach* do indeed share the responsibility of enlarging world population (ideally, filling the world with righteous individuals who live by God's Torah).[17]

Death

The rites of mourning over the death of close relatives are intended to give honor to the departed soul and to bring home the most basic fact of life that one's days in this physical realm are limited. As stated in Ecclesiastes:

> It is better to go to a house of mourning than to a house of merriment, for death is the destiny of every man; and the living will take it to heart.[18]

It is only when enclothed in flesh that we can choose to serve God and work to bring creation closer to its purpose, and our days are few. Mourning is a time for soul searching and re-commitment to dedicate all of our days on earth to the service of the One God of Israel.

Notes:

1. Genesis 2:9.
2. Proverbs 3:18,17. This is the order in which these two verses are recited when the Torah reading is concluded in a synagogue.
3. Deuteronomy 7:6 and 14:2.
4. Exodus 19:6.
5. See Maimonides *Hilchot Ma'achalot Asurot*, chapter 4.
6. *Bava Metzia* 58b.
7. The mysteries of creation are relevant to non-Jews as much as to Jews. However, the mysteries of God's infinite light before the beginning of the creative process are relevant only to Jews (and as such should not be taught to non-Jews or studied by them, just as with regard to the laws of the Torah that do not apply to non-Jews).
8. See in length in the introduction to *What You Need to Know About Kabbalah*, especially p. 8.
9. This is in accordance with the verse: "I will envision God through my flesh" (Job 19:26).
10. *Tana Debai Eliyahu*, chapter 9.
11. *Berachot* 35b.

12. *Likutei Moharan* II, 5:14.

13. Maimonides, *Hilchot Melachim* 10:9.

14. Alter Rebbe's *Shulchan Aruch, Orach Chayim* 2:8. See also *Avodah Zarah* 20b and *Shekalim* 9b.

15. Of Esau's third wife the sages learnt that though her real name was Bosmat (Genesis 36:3), at the time of her marriage she was called Mochalat (Genesis 28:9), which etymologically stems from the word meaning "forgiveness," because on one's wedding day a person repents and all of her or his sins are forgiven by God. See *Rashi* to Genesis 36:3. See also Jerusalem Talmud *Bikurim* 3:3 and *Midrash Shmu'el Rabati, parashah* 17.

16. "God Blessed them and said to them: Be fruitful and multiply; fill the earth and subdue it" (Genesis 1:28).

17. This is based on the verse: "He did not create it to be left desolate, He created it to be populated" (Isaiah 45:18). See *Shulchan Aruch Even Ha'ezer*, 1.

18. Ecclesiastes 7:2.

Unity Under God

6

Of the Holy Temple in Jerusalem God promised: "My house will be a house of prayer for all the nations."[1] *Bnei Noach* should pray to God that the Temple be rebuilt speedily in our days and encourage the Jewish people to do so.

History of the Temple

The site of the Temple—called *Har HaBayit*, the Temple Mount—is the holiest place on earth. According to tradition, Adam, the first man, was created from the earth of this very site. There Noah constructed an altar upon departing from the Ark.[2] It was there that Abraham brought his son Isaac as an offering to God.[3] This was where Jacob slept and dreamt of a ladder reaching straight to heaven.[4]

The holiness of this unique place was revealed to King David, who brought an offering there to God, and God responded with fire from heaven.[5] King David then bought the site from the Jebusites. And ever since then, the Temple Mount has been the eternal possession of the Jewish people.[6]

In the year 832 BCE, King Solomon built the Holy Temple there as a center for worshiping God, for adjudicating God's law, and for prayer. Solomon declared as follows:

> Whatever prayer or supplication be made by any individual or of all Your people Israel, each of

whom knows the affliction of his own heart, and spreading his hands toward this house.... Moreover concerning the foreigner that is not of Your people Israel, when he comes from a far country for Your Name's sake.... When he comes and prays toward this house, hear You in heaven Your dwelling place, and do according to all that the foreigner calls to You for.[7]

This house is the place that God chose for His Divine Presence to rest and become manifest, as the Book of Psalms states, "For God has chosen Zion; He has desired it for His habitation."[8]

The Temple that King Solomon built stood for 410 years, until it was destroyed by the Babylonians. Even during the seventy years of the Babylonian exile, the Jewish people retained their faith and devotion to the site. Sitting by the rivers of Babylon they swore, "If I forget you, O Jerusalem, let my right hand forget its skill...."[9] With the end of the Divinely decreed seventy-year exile, the Jewish people returned to the Land of Israel and Jerusalem and built the Temple a second time.

About 200 years after the construction of the Second Temple, the Land of Israel was overtaken by the Greeks. They took control of the Temple and of the priests serving there. They profaned the Holy of Holies—the innermost chamber of the Temple—and placed an idol in the courtyard of God's house. The conquerors' attempt to prevent the observance of Torah law and of services in the Temple greatly agitated the people of Israel. Led by the High Priest Mattathias and his son Judah the Maccabee, the Asmonean family spearheaded a rebellion against the Hellenistic empire.

The victory of the Asmoneans over the Greeks and the miracle that took place at that time—when the *menorah* stayed lit for eight days though only one cruise of pure olive oil could be found—are commemorated as the holiday of Hanukah. To this day, Jews celebrate Hanukah by lighting candles in their homes for eight days.

A few hundred years later, the land was once again conquered, this time by the Romans, whose oppressive regime likewise provoked a national rebellion. When this rebellion failed, the Romans destroyed the Second Temple, bringing to an end the living heart of the service of God. With the Temple's destruction, some 2,000 years ago, the Jewish people were once more exiled from the Land of Israel and dispersed amongst all the nations.

The Ninth Day of Av

Since then, the Holy Land has changed hands many times, yet throughout the generations, a small number of Jews always succeeded in keeping a foothold there. The day on which both the First and Second Temples were destroyed—the 9th day of the Hebrew month of *Av*—was marked as a special day of mourning. To this day, Jews the world over commemorate the day of the destruction of both Temples by fasting for a full twenty-four hours, sitting on the ground, weeping, and reciting the Book of Lamentations, Jeremiah's poem of mourning over the Temple's destruction, which contains the following words:

> Remember, O' GOD, what has come upon us;
> Behold, and see our reproach.
> Our inheritance has turned unto strangers,
> Our houses unto aliens....

The crown of our head has fallen;
Woe unto us for we have sinned.
For this our heart has become faint,
For these things our eyes have become dim:
For the mountain of Zion, which is desolate,
Foxes walk upon it.[10]

This profound lament concludes with a prayer of hope:

Return us to You, O' GOD, and we shall return.
Renew our days as of old.

Rebuilding the Temple and World Peace

The prophets of Israel, who envisioned the future redemption of Israel with the coming of the Messiah, declared that the Holy Temple would once more be rebuilt. These Divine prophecies instilled in the Jewish people the yearning, faith, and trust that Israel is destined to return to its former glory.

Faith in redemption, for Israel and for the entire world, is indeed one of the most important marks of Jewish culture, passing like a burning torch from generation to generation. Even now, in the period following the destruction of the Temple, Jews, regardless of where on earth they stand in prayer, face the Land of Israel, Jerusalem, and the Temple site, beseeching God to speedily reconstruct the Holy Temple.

The day is not far when God will accept our prayers and tears. In recent generations we have merited to witness the Divine Providence of the beginning of the return of the Jewish people to its homeland and to Jerusalem, the holy city. So too will we soon merit to witness the coming of the true Messiah and the reconstruction of the Temple, through which the Divine Presence will reside in our midst forever.

The Messiah will bring the word of God to all the nations of earth. The Divine light and truth inherent in his teachings will at once enlighten all humanity and bring about universal peace and blessing. Then, all nations will ascend to the Temple to serve the God of Israel, and behold of His Divine splendor. This has been foretold by the Prophet Isaiah:

> … out of Zion shall go forth the law,
> and the word of GOD from Jerusalem.
> And He shall judge between the nations,
> and instruct many peoples.
> And they shall hammer their swords into plowshares,
> and their spears into pruning hooks.
> Nation shall not lift up sword against nation,
> And never again will they learn war.[11]

From these words it is apparent that the seed of universal peace finds its fertile soil in the aspiration of all the nations of earth to worship the God of Israel in His Temple in Jerusalem.

According to the law of the Torah, which addresses both Jews and non-Jews, the Temple's holiness, which stems from God's eternal presence at this site, remains even when the Temple lies in ruin and foreign powers control the Temple Mount. This holiness thus obligates us to relate to the Temple Mount with supreme reverence, even today.

The Jewish people together with righteous gentiles the world over earnestly look forward to the coming of the Messiah and the return of the Divine Presence in all its majesty to this wondrous place, and recognize the holiness of what once was there, a holiness that still dwells hidden there like a glowing heart of fire inside a seemingly cold ember.

In heartfelt prayer to God, both Jew and righteous gentile can imagine themselves, in the inner eye of their souls, in the Holy Temple in Jerusalem. The Ba'al Shem Tov teaches that where one focuses his will and thought, that is where he really is.[12] From this holy place we beseech the Almighty to bring redemption to the entire world. In this way our prayers will be joined with the entreaties and yearning of all the generations of Israel, and we will merit abundant blessing from heaven.

How to Address Other Religions

Throughout this book we have repeatedly insisted that the Almighty does not condone the creation of religions. This is not to say that different nations and peoples cannot have local customs and rituals, but these should not include religious meaning and must be clearly differentiated from worship of the Divine.

However, today the world is full of so-called religious practice, which include various beliefs and rituals that have been set down as part of organized religions like Christianity and Islam. It is of these organized religions that many people are very suspicious, as it seems that they have been the cause of some of the greatest bloodshed and strife in human history. Instead of bringing peace to the human race they have dealt immeasurable suffering and little solace in times of grief.

Bnei Noach by definition renounce the Divine legitimacy of organized religions and resolve to worship God only as prescribed in the Torah. Nonetheless, as we will see, certain benefits have come from the religious consciousness that organized religions have brought to their believers. The valid parts of their religious consciousness can serve as a pivot point for approaching their religious leaders and arguing the necessity of following God's Will as revealed in the Torah.

As God-fearing people, we all believe that Divine Providence directs every detail of each and every one of our lives. Even when people choose to follow a certain course of action for their own reasons, it is God who is directing their steps from on high as He sees fit.[13] In most cases, this direction remains entirely hidden from human beings. In the words of King David, "Man's steps are established by GOD, and He desires his path."[14]

This principle is true for every detail of every individual's life, but it is immensely more prominent in the lives of those who have proven to be of crucial influence on the overall history of humanity. Here, too, there is both the individual's revealed, conscious intention that motivates his deeds and the hidden dimension, which is revealed only to God as He wondrously directs the fate of the world that He created to reveal therein His glory and infinite goodness.

Maimonides[15] writes of one whose life changed the course of history—Jesus of Nazareth—that he imagined that he was the messiah. He tried to actualize this, but failed. Instead of redeeming Israel and the entire world, his actions led to Israel being slain by the sword,[16] their remnant to be scattered and humiliated, the Torah to be altered, and the majority of the world to be deceived into serving a "god" other than the One God.[17]

Maimonides continues:

> Nevertheless, the intent of the Creator of the world is not within the power of man to comprehend, for [to paraphrase Isaiah 55:8] His ways are not our ways, nor are His thoughts our thoughts.

[Ultimately,] all the deeds of Jesus of Nazareth and the Ishmaelite who arose after him [i.e., Mohammed] will only serve to pave the way for the coming of the Messiah and for the improvement of the entire world, [motivating the nations] to serve God together, as it is written [Zephaniah 3:9], "For I shall then make the peoples pure of speech so that they will all call upon the Name of GOD and serve Him with one accord."

How will this come about? [As a result of these religions,] the entire world has already filled with talk of the Messiah, as well as of the Torah and the commandments. These matters have been spread among many [formerly] spiritually insensitive nations, who discuss these matters as well as the various commandments of the Torah. Some of them [i.e., the Christians] say: These commandments were true, but are not in force in the present age; they are not applicable for all time. Others [i.e., the Moslems] say: Implied in the commandments are hidden concepts that cannot be understood simply; the messiah has already come and revealed them.

[The stage is thus set so that] when the true Messianic king will arise and prove successful, his [position becoming] exalted and uplifted, they will all return and realize that their ancestors endowed them with a false heritage; their prophets and ancestors caused them to err.

Let us look at the situation of the world today. Nearly 2,000 years have passed since the establishment of the Christian religion. During these generations the suffering and pain of millions of people have not abated despite the great strides made by civilization, especially in the fields of science and technology. Every passing day, the heartfelt cry for God's salvation intensifies, the cry for the true and ultimate redemption to be ushered in by the Messiah. In the words of the Prophet Daniel (who according to the sages was worthy to have been the Messiah, had we merited it[18]): "How long until the end of these terrible things!"[19]

From the signs given us by the prophets and the sages, it appears most clearly that our generation is the generation to witness the final redemption. In order to hasten the coming of the true Messiah, we must endeavor to live in accordance with the new order he will establish. Although Maimonides seems to imply that this will happen only after the revelation of the Messiah, even now, in the moments before his arrival, we must try to "live with the Messiah," as though he is already with us (for indeed he walks amongst us, ready, more than ever before in history, to be revealed). And so, the time has come for the nations of the world, beginning with their religious leaders, to realize that their forefathers bequeathed them a false heritage.

The past 2,000 years have demonstrated the failure of all organized religions to live up to their self-proclaimed role of bearers of God's message of peace and unity. At the same time, a clearly unique Divine Providence has protected God's chosen people, the Jews, at once the most envied, scorned at, and persecuted people on earth, in their extended period of exile from the Land of Israel (because of their sins, and in order to uplift and gather fallen sparks from all four corners of the earth). Enlightened people around the world have acknowledged these two points.

It is now time that God's hidden intention, which has guided all of history to this day, be revealed to all. Only in this way can each and every individual sincerely acknowledge the truth and prepare himself or herself to greet the true Messiah, whose arrival, to redeem us all, is imminent.

It is the sacred duty of Jews together with *Bnei Noach* to fervently call upon enlightened and inspired religious leaders to acknowledge the truth! Your lead will be followed by the acknowledgment of all peoples of all religions.

All of us yearn for salvation. We are all aware of the terrible suffering throughout the world, and we all believe that the great goodness and joy humanity is destined to inherit will come with the arrival of the true Messiah. And since the essence of the Messiah's message is joy,[20] our return to the true faith in God's law—His Torah—can only be accomplished in joy (the joy of becoming close to God). Such a return will awaken the Messianic spirit within all humanity, and will culminate in the advent of the Messiah himself.

For the sake of God and for the sake of the goodness He promised to humanity, the time has come for all nations of the world and their religious leaders to make a radical transformation, to face reality candidly, abandon their former beliefs, and acknowledge the absolute truth! Imagine how gratified our One Father in heaven, our blessed Creator, will be to see such an unparalleled display of courage and dedication.

The greater one's influence on one's surroundings, the greater is one's responsibility. It is the sacred duty of every religious leader to enlighten and awaken the hearts of his followers to abandon the erroneous beliefs they have inherited from their forefathers, to undertake to follow the path of the righteous gentiles as defined by the Torah—to observe the seven Laws of *Bnei Noach* which God commanded to all humanity—and in joy and goodness of heart to prepare for the imminent coming of the true Messiah.

Notes:

1. Isaiah 56:7.

2. Maimonides, *Hilchot Beit Habechirah* 2:2.

3. Genesis, 22:4, 14; 2 Chronicles 3:1.

4. Genesis 28:12-22.

5. 1 Chronicles 21:26.

6. 2 Samuel 24:16-25; 1 Chronicles 21:15-30, 22:1-19.

7. 1 Kings 8:38-43.

8. Psalms 132:13.

9. Ibid. 137:5.

10. Lamentations 5:1-2,16-18.

11. Isaiah 2:3-4.

12. *Keter Shem Tov*, 56. Additionally, Chassidut focuses on the symbol of Noah's Ark as the highest utopian image of world peace and prosperity. Within the ark, there was an air of peace and harmony greater in some respects than even that achieved in the Holy Temple.

13. We believe that we do indeed possess free choice and that our deeds are not predetermined. Paradoxically, while omniscient, God does not determine our actions, and yet at the same time He does oversee and direct each and every detail of our lives. Our finite intelligence cannot reconcile this apparent contradiction— God knows all even before it takes place, yet allows us to choose freely—but our power of faith transcends our human reason. This is one of the basic tenets of Judaism.

14. Psalms 37:23.

15. Maimonides, *Hilchot Melachim* ch. 11.

16. Throughout the centuries, hundreds of thousands of Jews were murdered in the name of Christianity. The list of the atrocities is endless and includes blood-libels, pogroms, crusades, etc. These crimes were perpetrated with the intent that Jews must be forced to acknowledge and convert to the "true" religion.

17. Based upon the visions of the prophets and the teachings of the sages, Maimonides also outlines what the time of the Messiah will be like. He states that the Messiah will be a living Jew, a human being (the idea of a human-god is a completely pagan notion) descended from the house of David. He will become king of Israel, arouse the Jewish People to return to God and live by the way of the Torah, fight the enemies of Israel and be victorious, rebuild the Temple in Jerusalem, and bring all the Jews back from the Diaspora to the Land of Israel. He will continue to inspire the entire world to believe in the One God of Israel, and usher in an era of all human beings living together in peace, brotherhood, and prosperity. He will finally bring all of humanity (and even all of reality) to know God and cling to Him in truth.

18. *Sanhedrin* 98b. In Kabbalah, we are taught that in every generation there is one individual who is worthy to be the Messiah, if the generation so merits. Generally, this individual is not aware of his Messianic potential, though he feels the suffering of humanity and longs for the redemption of the world more than any other soul on earth. He senses more acutely than any other the need for himself and his brethren—the Jewish People and all of humankind—to return to God in truth. He leads his generation toward redemption with the inspiration that comes with the revelation of deeper and deeper dimensions of the Torah, especially as related to the times. He sees every current event as a prelude to the coming of the Messiah, a call to awaken and return, without fully realizing that he is the bearer of the Messianic potential. Indeed, we are taught that within each of our souls there exists a spark of the Messiah, which manifests as the cry—with total faith in God and His infinite goodness—for

redemption. Knowing that everyone possesses a spark of the Messiah makes it even harder for the Messiah of the generation to identify himself as the all-inclusive Messianic soul.

19. Daniel 12:6.

20. In Hebrew, the four letters of Messiah (מָשִׁיחַ) permute to spell the word for "he shall be happy" (יִשְׂמַח) or "he shall make others happy" (יְשַׂמֵּחַ). In Kabbalah, happiness is identified as the inner spiritual experience of understanding, the mother principle. As a mother eagle hovering over her offspring, so does the true experience of happiness hover above the normative state of created consciousness, waiting to fully enter the minds and hearts of all finite, created beings. This is the spiritual meaning of the coming of the Messiah to redeem all mankind.

Relating to the Jewish People　7

God chose the Jewish people to bring His light to the world. If the Jews possess a power that the non-Jews do not, it is not because of their own merit. It is simply a gift from God and must be used properly and never abused. This also means that, due to their expanded spiritual role, when the Jews fail in their mission they have more potential than non-Jews for exerting a negative influence on the world.

The mission of the Jewish people is to lovingly draw all the peoples of the earth to fulfill God's Will, which means to bring the entire world to recognize the One God and the truth of His law—the Torah. This is the sole absolute truth. The objective of peace and unity is that the entire world may come to believe exclusively in the One God of Israel, an important step in the redemption of the world. Then we will reach a state when all of humanity will worship the Creator together, "with one accord."[1] In the words of the prophet, "with one accord" reads literally "with one shoulder"; in the Torah, the "shoulder" symbolizes the acceptance of responsibility (as in "shouldering a burden."[2] In this state, every nation and every individual will willingly (as the Jewish people are commanded today) assume full responsibility to do their utmost to shine forth the light of God and to integrate the Divine light in all avenues of worldly endeavor. The goal will be to sanctify the mundane by dedicating all deeds to the Almighty.

Mankind's Unity and God's Oneness

The willingness of all people to truly "shoulder" the burden together with the Jewish people is the result of a powerful revelation of God's Oneness, which progressively becomes stronger as creation unfolds. In fact, the idiom "one shoulder" is part of a set of similar Biblical idioms (each beginning with the word "one...," echad, in Hebrew) that mark the progressive revelation of God's Oneness.

The first three idioms in this progression—"one day,"[3] "one place,"[4] and "one flesh"[5]—appear in the first two chapters of Genesis, and the fourth, "one shoulder," in the later prophets.[6] In Kabbalah, the three "ones" of creation correspond to the first three letters of God's essential Name *Havayah*: *yud*, *hei*, and *vav*. "Day" and "place," which symbolize time and space correspond to the letters *yud* (which corresponds to the *sefirah* of wisdom) and *hei* (which corresponds to the *sefirah* of understanding), while "flesh" corresponds to the *vav* (corresponding to the *sefirah* of beauty). Part of the reasoning behind this correspondence is that wisdom and understanding are considered inseparable; in the language of the *Zohar*, they are as "two companions that never part." Since the theory of relativity, we also see time and space as physically inseparable. The body, which is the subject of "one flesh," corresponds to the *sefirah* of beauty; in the language of the *Zohar*: "Beauty [is] the body."

Finally, the idiom "one shoulder," which symbolizes the future unity of all nations serving God together, corresponds to the final *hei* of *Havayah*, the letter that corresponds to the *sefirah* of kingdom, as it is written, "And GOD will be King over the whole world, on that day GOD will be One and His Name will be One."[7] The complete correspondence is thus:

letter of God's Name	Idiom	*sefirah*
yud	"one day"	wisdom
hei	"one place"	understanding
vav	"one flesh"	beauty
hei	"one shoulder"	kingdom

Let us meditate some more upon this correspondence. As noted above, these four idioms depict the progression of the revelation of the Almighty's unity. The first idiom "one day" constitutes the last two words of the Torah's five verse description of the first day of creation. The first word of the Torah's description is *"bereisheet"* (which is usually translated as: "In the beginning"). This word is closely associated with wisdom as in the verse: "The beginning of wisdom is the fear of GOD." In fact, the translation of the Torah into Aramaic[8] renders this word as "With wisdom [God created the heavens and the earth]." Literally, the word *"bereisheet"* is a reference to the beginning of "time," thus relating the *sefirah* of wisdom with time in a direct manner. In one commentary on the words "one day," the sages explain that the oneness revealed was that of God unto Himself, for He had not yet created any other consciousness, like that of the angels.

The second idiom, "one place," appears in the narrative of the third day and in reference to the separation of the higher waters from the lower waters described earlier in the second day of creation. Grammatically, the act of separating "between" any two things is linked to the *sefirah* of understanding.[9] A common Kabbalistic metaphor for the *sefirah* of understanding is that of a spacious hall into which the seminal consciousness of wisdom may enter. According to the sages, the angels were created on the second day, indicating that the oneness of "one place" is able to include more than that of the first day's.

The third idiom, "one flesh," describes the unity of man and woman. At this point, the scope of the revealed unity and oneness increases to where it is able to bridge the gap not only between God and the angels, but also between individual human beings, albeit those bonded by marriage. The bond between husband and wife is described elsewhere in the Bible as the "beauty of man,"[10] which again returns to the correspondence of this revelation of oneness with the letter *vav* of God's essential Name.

The full verse from which the phrase "one shoulder" is taken reads: "For then I will transform the nations to speak one clear language in order to declare GOD's Name, to serve Him with one shoulder [accord]." The image used to describe the unity of the nations is that of a servant serving his king. When the servant submits himself completely before God and His Will, he merits being transformed himself into a king, for "the [true] servant of a king, is a king himself."[11] Furthermore, the three letters of the word "shoulder" (שְׁכֶם) in Hebrew are an acronym for the phrase "the glorious Name of His kingdom," (שֵׁם כְּבוֹד מַלְכוּתוֹ) clearly relating it to the *sefirah* of kingdom. At this level, the revelation of God's oneness is powerful enough to unite the consciousness of all mankind — not only husband and wife are bound together in their service of the Almighty but entire nations—a vision that truly reveals the majesty of the Almighty.

The average value of the four phrases is 289 or 17^2, the value of "[In the beginning] God created...." The Almighty created the world in order to reveal His absolute unity in all, as manifest in the four "ones," depicting the absolute unity that is inherent in each of the four letters of His essential Name.[12] When this unity occurs, the final redemption will come.[13]

Our Highest Common Denominator

The world at this time is in a state of plurality, not unity. The plethora of churches, temples, and mosques in every town reflects this plurality. Just to say that "we are all human, so we are all one" expresses nothing more than our lowest common denominator (otherwise called "the human condition"). But, making do with our lowest common denominator cannot replace the true goal of humanity, which is to achieve real unity by expressing our highest aspirations and realizing our deepest potentials.

Real unity is based upon the knowledge of one absolute Divine truth and one source of Divine revelation to which all the peoples of the earth subscribe. Only this state of consciousness and commitment can create true unity in the world, permeating all the interactions between individuals and nations. In our prayers to God for "peace on earth"[14] we must first beseech Him that all of mankind gain knowledge of the One.[15] By knowing (i.e., recognizing the presence of) God wherever we turn in our daily chores we redeem Divine sparks from the prison of mundane reality. Only after all the sparks have been redeemed can peace come to the world.[16]

Holy and Separate

It is of utmost importance that while the Jews are fulfilling their special mission, the Jewish core remains holy and separate. The Torah refers to the Jewish people as "a nation that dwells alone."[17] This separation is not meant to condone plurality, but rather to ensure that the Jewish nation remains holy and strong while it accomplishes its purpose to become a beacon of faith, which shines its light to the entire world and attracts all. Ultimately, all the people of the earth will come to worship the One God, but without the Jewish people, the world cannot reach a state of unity.

The essential statement of monotheism as proclaimed in the Torah is: "Hear O' Israel, GOD is our God, GOD is One."[18] In the future, with the coming of the Messiah, "GOD is One" will be obvious at last to all,[19] as the Prophet Zechariah proclaims, "And GOD will be King over the whole world, on that day GOD will be One and His Name will be One."[20]

Until that time comes, the on-going task of the Jews as a nation of priests is to help non-Jews achieve their spiritual state of rectification.

Perfecting the world is up to all of humanity—it is a process whereby, through our actions we spiritually liberate and retrieve the fragments of Divine light trapped within the material realm, as mentioned above. By elevating these fragments of Divine light from the physical reality into which they fell, we gradually achieve a rectification of the world and restore it to its initially intended state of perfection in the unity of the One God.

For the Jews to succeed in this task, non-Jews must realize that a general tenet applies to the relationship between the Jew and the non-Jew upon which the very rectification of the world depends. That is, non-Jews cannot be considered righteous gentiles if in their hearts they do not recognize the authority of the Torah and feel no affinity to God's chosen people (whom the Torah identifies as such). This is true regardless of how many good deeds the non-Jews perform as a group or as individuals and no matter what fine character traits they possess.[21]

When non-Jews possess a sense of affinity towards Jews, they draw inspiration from the source of the soul of Israel. They become motivated to be good people in all relations with others and to devote their lives to the service of God. The rectification of the non-Jewish world depends upon the inspiration and insight it receives from the Jewish people in its role as "a nation of priests."[22]

Affinity to Every Jew

But even when the non-Jewish world at large does not yet possess conscious affinity and subordinance to the Jewish people, it is still possible for us to extract a spark of goodness from the shell of evil. For example, the major religion of Western culture believes in an individual Jew and worships him as a god. This is certainly a great transgression of the most fundamental of the *Bnei Noach* commandments, the commandment that forbids idolatry (as noted earlier). But within this evil context we can perceive an element of good. The believers in this religion desire, whether consciously or unconsciously, to cling to a Jew for inspiration and salvation.[23]

The true rectification of the non-Jewish world will come when it recognizes the Divinely ordained purpose of *every* Jew to enlighten the world and bring about universal peace and prosperity as has been prophesized. The non-Jew will then be drawn, in love, to the Jew.

With an existential feeling of attachment to the Jewish people—who in their own consciousness represent the epitome of lowliness before God and man—the world will acknowledge the obligations of the Kingdom of Heaven as explained in the Torah. The nations of the world will then merit true insight and partake in the ultimate redemption.

Notes:

1. Zephaniah 3:9.
2. See also Genesis 49:15.
3. Ibid. 1:5.
4. Ibid. 1:9.
5. Ibid. 2:24.
6. The numerical values of the three idioms in Genesis are 69, 199, 515, respectively. When the numerical value of "one shoulder," 373, is added to these, the sum equals 1156 or 34^2. When the numerical sum of a number of related concepts is a square number, this indicates that together they form a complete or consummate set.
7. Zachariah 14:9.
8. Known as *Targum Yerushalmi*.
9. See *What You Need to Know About Kabbalah*, p. 87.
10. Isaiah 44:13.
11. *Shvu'ot* 47b.
12. The four idioms in Hebrew are: יוֹם אֶחָד, מָקוֹם אֶחָד, בָּשָׂר אֶחָד and שְׁכֶם אֶחָד. Together they contain $25 = 5^2$ letters (see also note 18) and can therefore be drawn in square form, as follows:

ח	א	ם	ו	י
ם	ו	ק	מ	ד
שׁ	ב	ד	ח	א
שׁ	ד	ח	א	ר
ד	ח	א	ם	כ

In this configuration, the middle letter is ד, which is equal to 4, or 2^2. The sum of the 8 letters surrounding the middle letter is 169, or 13^2 (13 is the numerical value of the word "one," אֶחָד, itself):

ו	ק	מ
ב		ח
ד	ח	א

Finally, the sum of the rest of the letters is 983:

$$
\begin{array}{ccccc}
\text{ה} & \text{א} & \text{ם} & \text{ו} & \text{׳} \\
\text{ם} & & & & \text{ד} \\
\text{שׁ} & & & & \text{א} \\
\text{שׁ} & & & & \text{ר} \\
\text{ד} & \text{ה} & \text{א} & \text{ם} & \text{כ} \\
\end{array}
$$

What we have done is identified a 3 stage geometric progression in the square configuration—from the middle letter to the first square the surrounds it to the second square that surrounds them both. The three values in our progression are 4, 169, and 983, which can be used to develop a quadratic series (see glossary). The sum of the first 7 terms of this series is 26208 = 91 · 288. In Kabbalah, 91 represents a complex oneness, as it is the sum of all integers from 1 to 13 (13 is the numerical value of the word "one," אֶחָד, in Hebrew), written △13. 288 is the number of sparks of Divine holiness that fell into mundane reality at the beginning of creation. The fallen state of these 288 sparks is one of the primary reasons that we retain our disunified perception of the Almighty and of reality. By recognizing God's unity in all and committing ourselves to serve Him in unity in order to bring the world to its ultimate state of rectification, we are able to elevate, or redeem the sparks of holiness and all of mundane reality.

13. This is what is meant in the *Zohar* (III, 124b) that by revealing the sweet teachings of the *Zohar*, the mysteries of the Torah, the final redemption will come with loving-kindness and mercy. As such, consciousness of the One God (the essence of all the teachings of the *Zohar* and all subsequent texts of Kabbalah and Chassidut) must precede the final redemption. Otherwise, the redemption will certainly tarry and it will be accompanied with hardship and suffering.

14. *Rabbeinu Yonah's* commentary to *Mishnah Avot* 3:2. See Rebbe Nachman of Breslov's *Likutei Tefilot* II, 34, and in many other places.

15. Just as the first request made in the *Amidah* is for knowledge and consciousness.

16. *Tanya, Igeret Hakodesh* 12 (page 234).

17. Numbers 23:9.

18. Deuteronomy 6:4. Like the four idioms of "oneness" discussed above, this verse also has exactly 25 letters and can also be drawn as a 5 by 5 square whose mathematical analysis has been carried out elsewhere.

19. *Rashi* explains that God will be one as "all the nations will refute their gods, therefore God alone will remain without false gods."

20. Zechariah 14:9.

21. According to the ruling of the Brisker Rav, one of the previous generation's greatest legal authorities, non-Jews (no matter how cultured they may appear to be) who hate Jews to the extent that they have sworn to destroy them, are considered part of the nation of Amalek. Amalek was and continues to be the archenemy of Israel, whom the Jewish people are commanded by God to annihilate (Deuteronomy 25:17-19; see also Exodus 17:14-16). Their hatred of the Jewish people is actually their hatred of God, as explicitly stated in the Torah. These enemies of God and the Jewish people are the subject of Moses' declaration: "Rise O' GOD and Your enemies will disperse and those who hate You will flee from You" (Numbers 11:35). *Rashi* explains that "those who hate You" are those who hate the Jewish people. As we all know, this is not a story of the distant past, but one of the present, as exemplified by Nazi Germany and Arab terrorists.

22. Exodus 19:6.

23. For this very reason, many Arian philosophers (at the turn of the last century) abandoned Christianity (preferring previous pagan beliefs), unwilling to bear the fact the Jesus was a Jew (yet others compromised that his father was a Roman soldier, endowing him, though a bastard, with Arian blood).

Glossary

Note: all foreign terms are Hebrew unless otherwise indicated. Terms preceded by an asterisk have their own entries.

30 Laws of *Bnei Noach*: based on the Talmud, initially, *Bnei Noach* wanted to accept 30 commandments. Most Jewish legal authorities understand that the 30 are the next logical expansion of the original 7 Laws of *Bnei Noach*.

acknowledgment: see *sefirot*.

Action: see Worlds.

Adam Kadmon: see *partzufim*.

aiver min hachai: lit., a limb from that which is alive. Jews and non-Jews alike are prohibited from eating it. This prohibition is one of the seven Laws of *Bnei Noach*.

alef: letter of the *Hebrew Alphabet

Amidah (עֲמִידָה, "standing"): the central core and highest point of every prayer service. It is recited as a silent devotion while standing, feet together, facing Jerusalem. The weekday version consists of nineteen blessings; the *Shabbat* and holiday versions consist of seven, and the version of the *Musaf* of *Rosh HaShanah* consists of nine.

Animal soul: the lower soul of the human being, so named for its similarity to the animating life-force of animals. See also *beinoni*, *Tanya*.

Aramaic: the international language spoken in the Middle East and adopted widely by the Jewish people from the end of the First Temple era (c. 4th century BCE) to the conclusion of the editing of the Talmud (c. 5th century CE). Mystically, it is considered to be the closest language to the Holy Language (Biblical Hebrew). Many

183

basic Jewish texts, such as the Talmud and the *Zohar*, require a working knowledge of Aramaic to be studied in the original.

Arizal: Luria, Rabbi Yitzchak (1534-1572): central figure of Kabbalah, whose teachings form the core of Kabbalistic doctrine and the basis for understanding the *Zohar*. Known by the acronym *Arizal* (אֲרִיזַ"ל): הָאֱלֹקִי רַבֵּינוּ יִצְחָק זִכְרוֹנוֹ לִבְרָכָה, "the G-dly Rabbi Yitzchak [Luria Ashkenazi], of blessed memory."

Asiyah (Action): see Worlds.

Asmonean family (*Chashmona'im*): the offspring of Mattathias the High Priest who led a successful revolt of the Jewish people in the Land of Israel against the Greek Seleucid dynasty and local Hellenists in the 2nd century BCE. The Asmoneans founded an autonomous Jewish state that lasted from 140 BCE to 37 BCE.

Atik Yomin: see *partzufim*.

Atzilut (Emanation): see Worlds.

Av: the 5th month of the Jewish Year, coinciding approximately with August.

ayin: letter of the *Hebrew Alphabet.

Ba'al Shem Tov (בַּעַל שֵׁם טוֹב, "Master of the Good Name [of God]"): title of Rabbi Yisrael ben Eliezer (1698-1760), founder of the Chassidic movement (see *Chassidut*).

beauty: see *sefirot*.

behavioral powers: the *sefirot* victory, acknowledgment, and foundation.

Beinoni (בֵּינוֹנִי, "intermediate"): someone who still possesses an evil urge but controls it and does not sin. There are many levels of *beinoni*, from the one who is in a continuous conscious state of battle in order to overcome his evil inclination, to the one so engrossed in his Divine service of Torah and *mitzvot* that he is virtually unaware of the evil inclination dormant in him. See also *tzadik*.

beit: letter of the *Hebrew Alphabet.

Ben Noach: Hebrew. Masculine singular form of *Bnei Noach*, meaning "son of Noah."

Bat Noach: Hebrew. Feminine singular form of *Bnei Noach*, meaning "daughter of Noah."

Beriah (Creation): see Worlds.

birur (בֵּרוּר, "clarification," "separation," "choosing," or "refinement"): a type of *tikun* in which one must work to separate good from evil in any given entity, and then reject the evil and accept the good (a process known as "elevating sparks"). This may be done actively or in one's consciousness. See also *klipat nogah, yichud*.

Blessings: the Torah commands that one bless the Almighty after eating meals. One of the seven commandments instituted by the sages is the recital of blessings before and after all foods, before the performance of a *mitzvah* and upon encountering or experiencing certain wonders of the human and natural world.

Bnei Noach (lit.,"children of Noah"): the Talmudic connotation for non-Jews that follows the seven universal commandments given to Adam and Noah.

Bnei Yisrael (lit., "children of Israel"): the connotation of the Jewish people throughout most of the *Bible.

Canaan: 1. Name of Noah's grandson, the son of Cham (identified by the sages as Eliezer, Abraham's servant). See also Land of Canaan.

Chabad: 1. Acronym for the names of the three *intellectual *sefirot: *chochmah, binah,* and *da'at* (wisdom, understanding, and knowledge); 2. The branch of *Chassidut founded by Rabbi Shneur Zalman of Liadi (1745-1812), emphasizing the role of the intellect and meditation in the service of God.

Chassidut ("piety," or "loving-kindness"): 1. An attribute or way of life that goes beyond the letter of the law. 2. The movement of Jewish spiritual renewal founded by Rabbi Yisrael Ba'al Shem Tov (1648-1760), the purpose of which is to awaken the Jewish people to its own inner self through the inner dimension of the Torah and thus to prepare the way for the advent of the *Messiah. 3. The oral and written teachings of this movement.

chirik: vowel sign in Hebrew; see *Hebrew Alphabet.

cholam: vowel sign in Hebrew; see *Hebrew Alphabet.

Circumcision (*milah*, in Hebrew): 1. The rite performed on a Jewish boy on the eighth day after his birth. 2. Specifically, the first phase of this rite in which the foreskin is cut.

clarification: see *birur*.

commandments: see *mitzvah*.

concealed brain (*mocha stima'a*): part of the mystical anatomy of the *sefirah of crown, which represents the unconscious reasoning behind human will.

confidence: see *sefirot*.

Congregation of Israel (*kneset Yisrael*): the source and consummate vessel of all the souls of the Jewish people.

Cordovero, Rabbi Moshe: see *Pardes Rimonim*.

correspondence: the literal meaning of the word "Kabbalah," in the Five Books of Moses. It is the main tool of contemplative Jewish mysticism.

covenant: a bond made between two sides that is beyond reason and independent of future events and states.

covenant numbers: the series of integer numbers that are produced by the function $f[n] = n^2 ⊥ n ⊥ 1$. Figuratively, can be drawn as two triangles joined by a single point.

Creation: see Worlds.

crown: see *sefirot*.

daily prayers: morning, afternoon, and evening prayer services. They were instituted by the *patriarchs and correspond to the daily sacrifice service in the *Holy Temple. On holidays a fourth prayer service is added and on *Yom Kipur, there are five prayers services. Mystically, there are seven time slots for prayer during the day, which also include a prayer service before sleep and a prayer service at midnight.

dalet: letter of the *Hebrew Alphabet.

Days of the Messiah (*yemot hamashi'ach*): the era beginning with the coming of the *Messiah. In many sources it is described as lasting 40 years, that will either coincide or lead up to the two eras of the building of the Holy *Temple in Jerusalem and/or the resurrection of the dead, each of which is also described as lasting 40 years.

Divine Presence (*shechinah*): the term used to describe the Almighty's mundane and immanent Presence, which can be given full expression only in the Holy *Temple in Jerusalem.

Divine Providence (*hashgachah*): the term used to describe the Almighty's knowledge, awareness, and guidance of creation.

Divine soul: the higher soul which is considered, in essence, to be a part of the Almighty. See also animal soul, *Tanya*.

Elokim: see Names of God.

Emanation: see Worlds.

emotional powers: refers to the three *sefirot* loving-kindness, might, and beauty.

Esau: Jacob's twin brother who founded the nation of Edom. In Rabbinic writings, Edom is considered to have melted into the Roman Empire.

eternity: see *sefirot*.

evolution of worlds (*seder hishtalshelut*): the Kabbalistic description of the stages in the process of creation discussed primarily in the writings of the *Arizal* and *Chabad*.

faith: see *sefirot*.

fear: see *sefirot*.

finite differences: a mathematical technique used to extend series of integer numbers by finding the base of the series.

Formation, see Worlds.

foundation: see *sefirot*.

fulfillment: see *sefirot*.

gematria (geometric-numerical value [Aramaic]): the technique of comparing Hebrew words and phrases based on their numerical values. For a more complete discussion see Appendix 1 to *The Mystery of Marriage*.

ger toshav (resident alien): The status of a non-Jew who has committed to upholding the seven *Laws of *Bnei Noach* before a court of Jewish law (a *Beit Din*). Such a *Ben Noach* is then permitted to reside in the Land of Israel. There are differing Halachic opinions regarding the applicability of this status in our times.

God's signature: the Talmud states that the Almighty signs His essential Name, *Havayah*, as it were, within every aspect of creation, much like an artist signs his name on a piece of art. This motivates us to search for God's essential Name, *Havayah* in everything that we study. Rabbi Yitzchak Ginsburgh's Hebrew volume *Sod Hashem Liyerei'av* is dedicated to this mystical pursuit.

Halachah: Torah law.

halachic authority: an individual recognized as an authority in the area of Torah law.

Havayah: see Names of God.

head covering (*kipah* [Hebrew], *yarmulke* [Yiddish]): the traditional Jewish head covering for men, manifests one's fear and awe of Heaven.

Hebrew Alphabet: known after its first two letters as the *Alef beit* (אָלֶף בֵּית)—comprises twenty-two letters, five of which possess a secondary form used at the end of a word. These letters are all consonants. Vowels are generally indicated as diacritical marks underneath, above, or after the letters; however, four of the twenty-two consonants (the letters: א ה ו י) indicate vowel-sounds as well

	letter	name		Sound		letter	name		Sound
1	א	אָלֶף	alef	'	12	ל	לָמֶד	lamed	l
2	ב	בֵּית	beit	b, v	13	מ, ם	מֵם	mem	m
3	ג	גִּימֶל	gimel	g	14	נ, ן	נוּן	nun	n
4	ד	דָלֶת	dalet	d	15	ס	סָמֶךְ	samech	s
5	ה	הֵא	hei	h	16	ע	עַיִן	ayin	'
6	ו	וָו	vav	v	17	פ, ף	פֵּא	pei	p, f
7	ז	זַיִן	zayin	z	18	צ, ץ	צָדִי	tzadi	tz
8	ח	חֵית	chet	ch	19	ק	קוּף	kuf	k
9	ט	טֵית	tet	t	20	ר	רֵישׁ	reish	r
10	י	יוּד	yud	y	21	שׁ	שִׁין	shin	sh, s
11	כ, ך	כָּף	kaf	k, ch	22	ת	תָו	tav	t

The diacritical vowel marks (called *neekud*, in Hebrew) are:

	mark	name		sound		mark	name		sound
1	ָ	קָמַץ	kamatz	ah	5	ְ	שְׁבָא	sh'va	' e
2	ַ	פַּתַח	patach	ah	6	וֹ	חוֹלָם	cholam	o
3	ֵ	צֵירֶה	tzaireh	ai	7	ִ	חִירִיק	chirik	ee
4	ֶ	סֶגוֹל	segol	e	8	ֻ	קֻבּוּץ	kubootz	oo

	mark	name		sound
9	וּ	שׁוּרֻק	shoorook	oo
10	ָ:	חֲטָף קָמֵץ	chataf kamatz	ah

	mark	name		sound
11	ֲ	חֲטָף פַּתַח	chataf patach	ah
12	ֱ	חֲטָף סֶגּוֹל	chataf segol	e

hei: letter of the *Hebrew Alphabet.

Hillel the Elder (*Hilel Hazaken*): 1st century sage who came from Babylon to the Land of Israel. He was a direct descendant of the House of King David and the founder of the institution of the *Nasi* (lit., "the exalted"), who served as the head of the *Sanhedrin. His scholarly disputant was *Shamai*.

humility: see *sefirot*.

intellectual powers: the *sefirot* wisdom, understanding, and knowledge.

intellectual soul (*nefesh sichlit*): the intermediary soul between the Divine and animal souls.

inter-inclusion (*hitkalelut*): a principle of Kabbalistic thought whereby every part of a whole contains the entire whole. Physically, this principle is best exhibited in a hologram and therefore is also known as the holographic principle.

intermediate shell (*klipat nogah*): lies between the sacred aspects of a *World and its three impure shells. Elements contained in it are considered to have sparks of Divine holiness, which can be elevated, i.e., freed, through the service of *clarification.

Isaac: the son of *Abraham and Sarah and the second patriarch of the Jewish people.

Ishmael: the son of *Abraham and Hagar—Sarah's maidservant. The father of the Arabian peoples.

Jacob: the son of Isaac and Rivkah (Rebecca). Twin brother to *Esau and the third patriarch of the Jewish people. Had 12 children who became the Tribes of Israel.

Jebusites: the Canaanite nation that lived in the city of Yevus (Jebus) before it was conquered by King David and made into his capitol of Jerusalem.

Kabbalah: the mystical tradition of the *Torah.

kamatz: vowel sign in Hebrew; see *Hebrew Alphabet.

kav: the ray of infinite light inserted into the void created by the *tzimtzum* and out of which emanated the *World of *Adam Kadmon*; considered one of the stages in the *evolution of worlds.

kingdom: see *sefirot*.

klipat nogah: see intermediate shell.

Kneset Yisrael: see Congregation of Israel.

knowledge: see *sefirot*.

Land of Canaan: the first name of the Land of Israel, so named for the seven Canaanite nations that inhabited it. In *Chassidut, refers to the seven powers of the *animal soul. See also *Canaan.

Land of Israel: the land that the Almighty promised to *Bnei Yisrael*.

light, God's: the Kabbalistic term used to describe God's revelation in the *Worlds.

love: see *sefirot*.

loving-kindness: see *sefirot*.

Lubavitcher Rebbe: 1. One of the seven leaders of *Chabad-Lubavitch. 2. Specifically, the last Rebbe, Rabbi Menachem Mendel Schneersohn (1902-1994).

Mashiach, see Messiah.

mercy: see *sefirot*.

Messiah (lit., "anointed one"): the prophesied descendant of King David who will reinstate the *Torah-ordained monarchy (which he will head), rebuild the Holy *Temple, and gather the exiled Jewish people to their homeland. This series of events (collectively called "the Redemption," or "*ge'oolah*," in Hebrew) will usher in an era of eternal, universal peace and true knowledge of God, called the *messianic era.

messianic era: see Days of the Messiah.

might: see *sefirot*.

mitzvah ("commandment"; pl., *mitzvot*): 1. One of the 613 commandments given by God to the Jewish people, or 7 commandments given by God to the nations of the world, at Mt. Sinai. 2. One of the seven commandments instituted by the sages. 3. Idiomatically, any good deed.

mitzvot: plural of **mitzvah*.

Mt. Sinai: location where God gave the Torah.

Names of God: Any of the seven sanctified words used to refer to the Almighty. For a complete reference see Appendix 2 of **The Mystery of Marriage* and part III of **What You Need to Know About Kabbalah*.

netilat yadayim (lit., "taking the hands"): ritual purifying washing of the hands upon waking up in the morning, before eating bread, or after the hands are made impure for various reasons. The vessel from which water is poured onto the hands is called a *natla*.

Nineveh: the capitol of the Assyrian empire in Biblical times, to which the prophet **Jonah was sent.

Noahide covenant: the covenant made between God and Noah and all of his offspring after the Flood, and the basis for humanity's relationship with the Almighty since then. On the one hand God will never again destroy the world with a flood, on the other, humanity will commit to upholding the seven **Laws of Bnei Noach*. The sign of the covenant was the rainbow.

Laws of *Bnei Noach*: the set of seven commandments given to Adam, the first human being, and then reiterated as part of the **Noahide covenant. They are: 1. Prohibition of idolatry, 2. Prohibition of adultery, 3. Prohibition of murder, 4. Prohibition of theft, 5. Prohibition of blasphemy, 6. prohibition of eating a limb from a live animal, and 7. An injunction to set up a just legal system. Each of the commandments is considered to be general with many particular laws stemming from each.

parashah ("section"; pl. *parashiot*): 1. A paragraph in the written Torah according to the Masoretic text. These *parshiot* are either "open" (followed by a blank space which extends to the end of the line) or "closed" (followed by a blank space equal to the width of nine letters). 2. One of the fifty-four sections into which the Five Books of Moses are divided (also called a *sidrah*, lit., "order") for the purpose of reading one of them in the synagogue each **Shabbat*. Thus, the entire Torah is read in full in the course of a year (it is sometimes necessary to read two on the same Sabbath). The *parshiot* are known by one or two of their opening words.

partzuf (lit., "persona"; pl. *partzufim*): the third and final stage in the development of a **sefirah*, in which it metamorphoses from a tenfold articulation of sub-*sefirot* into a human-like figure possessing the full set of intellectual and emotional powers. As such, it may thus interact with the other *partzufim* (which could not occur before this transformation. This stage of development constitutes the transition from **tohu* to **tikun* (or from *Nekudim* to *Berudim*, see Worlds).

The **sefirot* develop into a primary and a secondary array of *partzufim*, as follows:

sefirah	primary *partzufim*		secondary *partzufim*	
crown	עַתִּיק יוֹמִין Atik Yomin	"The Ancient of Days"	עַתִּיק יוֹמִין Atik Yomin	[The male dimension of] "the Ancient of Days"
			נוּקְבֵיה דְעַתִּיק יוֹמִין Nukvei d'Atik Yomin	[The female dimension of] "the Ancient of Days"
	אֲרִיךְ אַנְפִּין Arich Anpin	"The Long Face"	אֲרִיךְ אַנְפִּין Arich Anpin	[The male dimension of] "the Long Face"
			נוּקְבֵיה דְאֲרִיךְ אַנְפִּין Nukvei d'Arich Anpin	[The female dimension of] "the Long Face"
wisdom	אַבָּא Abba	"Father"	אַבָּא עִילָאָה Abba Ila'ah	"Supernal Father"
			אִמָּא עִילָאָה Ima Ila'ah	"Supernal Mother"
understanding	אִמָּא Ima	"Mother"	יִשְׂרָאֵל סַבָּא Yisrael Saba	"Israel the Elder"
			תְּבוּנָה Tevunah	"Understanding"
loving-kindness thru foundation	זְעֵיר אַנְפִּין Z'eir Anpin	"The Small Face"	יִשְׂרָאֵל Yisrael	"Israel"
			לֵאָה Leah	"Leah"
kingdom	נוּקְבֵיה דִזְעֵיר אַנְפִּין Nukvei d'Z'eir Anpin	"The Female of Z'eir Anpin"	יַעֲקֹב Yaakov	"Jacob"
			רָחֵל Rachel	"Rachel"

Both of the secondary, male and female *partzufim* of *Atik Yomin* and *Arich Anpin* exist within the same figure. There are thus actually only ten distinct secondary *partzufim*.

Within any particular *partzuf*, the *sefirot* are arranged along three axes, right, left and middle, as follows:

left axis	center axis	right axis
	crown	
understanding		wisdom
	knowledge	
might		loving-kindness
	beauty	
acknowledgment		victory
	foundation	
	kingdom	

In this arrangement, there are three triads of related *sefirot*: wisdom-understanding-knowledge (the intellect), loving-kindness-might-beauty (the primary emotions) and victory-acknowledgment-foundation (the behavioral attributes).

Passover: Seven (eight in the Diaspora) day holiday commencing on the 15th day of Nisan and commemorating the Exodus from Egypt.

patriarchs: the fathers of the Jewish people: *Abraham, *Isaac, and *Jacob. Kabbalistically, every Jewish soul contains their essential qualities.

pleasure: see *sefirot*.

Priestly Blessing: the three verse blessing (Numbers 6:24-26) that Aaron and his offspring, the Jewish priesthood, recite as commanded by God.

pyramid numbers: integer numbers that are produced by the function $f[n] = \sum_{0}^{n} \Sigma^2$.

Rabbi: Title conferred on one who has proven dedication to and knowledge of the *Torah, specifically to *Halachah*.

Responsa: genre of Halachic literature that includes questions asked of Halachic authorities and the responses given to these queries.

righteous gentile: synonym for a *Ben* or *Bat Noach*.

righteous individual: see *tzadik*.

Rosh Hashanah: the first two days of the Jewish year, commemorating the creation of Adam and day of universal Divine judgment.

Sefirah (pl., *sefirot*): a channel of Divine energy or life force. It is via the *sefirot* that God interacts with creation; they may thus be considered His "attributes."

There are altogether eleven *sefirot* spoken of in Kabbalistic literature. Inasmuch as two of them (crown and knowledge) are two dimensions of a single force, the tradition generally speaks of only ten *sefirot*. Each *sefirah* also possesses an inner facet that can be experienced directly, as discussed in *Chassidut*. The order of the *sefirot* is depicted in the following chart:

name			inner experience	
keter	כֶּתֶר	crown	אֱמוּנָה תַּעֲנוּג רָצוֹן	faith pleasure will
chochmah	חָכְמָה	wisdom	בִּטוּל	selflessness
binah	בִּינָה	understanding	שִׂמְחָה	joy
da'at	דַּעַת	knowledge	יִחוּד	union
chesed	חֶסֶד	loving-kindness	אַהֲבָה	love
gevurah	גְּבוּרָה	strength, or might	יִרְאָה	fear, or awe
tiferet	תִּפְאֶרֶת	beauty	רַחֲמִים	mercy
netzach	נֶצַח	victory, or eternity	בִּטָחוֹן	confidence
hod	הוֹד	acknowledgment, or thanksgiving	תְּמִימוּת	sincerity, or earnestness
yesod	יְסוֹד	foundation	אֱמֶת	truth, or fulfillment
malchut	מַלְכוּת	kingdom	שִׁפְלוּת	lowliness

Originally emanated as simple point-like forces, the *sefirot* at a certain stage develop into *inter-inclusive spectrums of ten sub-*sefirot*. Subsequent to this, they metamorphose into *partzufim*.

Sefirot are composed of "lights" and "vessels." The light of any *sefirah* is the Divine flow within it; the vessel is the identity that flow takes in order to relate to or create some aspect of the world in a specific way. Inasmuch as all reality is created by means of the *sefirot*, they constitute the conceptual paradigm for understanding all reality.

sefirot: plural of *sefirah*.

service of clarifications: see *birur*.

service of unifications: see *yichud*.

Shabbat ("Sabbath"): the day of rest beginning at sunset on Friday and ending at nightfall on Saturday. Non-Jews, including *Bnei Noach*, are forbidden to keep the Shabbat in its Halachic sense.

shells of impurity (*kelipot*): every *world contains four shells initially meant to safeguard it in its immature state. Once the *world has reached maturity, the shells that continue to envelop it are considered impure, inasmuch as they prevent God's light from penetrating. Three shells are considered completely impure and crippling and cannot be rectified, while one, the *intermediate shell, acts as an intermediary between the *world and the three impure shells and is rectified by either *birur* or *yichud*.

Shema (שְׁמַע, "hear"): a compilation of three Biblical passages (*Deuteronomy* 6:4-9, 11:13-21, *Numbers* 15:37-41) beginning with this word, or sometimes, the first verse alone. The first verse is the fundamental profession of monotheism, "Hear O Israel, GOD is our God, GOD is one." We are commanded to recite the *Shema* twice daily, and it has been incorporated into the morning and evening services as well as the prayer said upon retiring at night. When reciting the first sentence, we are intended to consider ourselves ready to give up our lives rather than deny the oneness of God.

shofar ("ram's horn"): the *shofar* was blown (by God) at the giving of the Torah, is blown (by man) every *Rosh HaShanah* in fulfillment of G-d's commandment, expressing contrition and penitence, and will be again blown (by God) at the beginning of the Redemption to herald the arrival of *Mashiach*.

shva: vowel sign in Hebrew; see *Hebrew Alphabet.

sincerity: see *sefirot*.

Sivan: the third month of the Jewish year.

something from nothing: description given to the Creation of reality. "Nothing" implies both that which is not as well as that which is incomprehensible to the human mind. Also referred to as "ex nihilo."

soul-root: a common spiritual source of many souls co-existing in a single generation.

sparks: Divinity as it appears to give life to a mundane entity.

super-conscious: refers to the *sefirah of crown and its constituent *partzufim and the corresponding experiential faculties.

supernal heads of the crown: see *sefirot*.

Temple (also Holy Temple, *Beit Hamikdash*, in Hebrew): the central sanctuary in Jerusalem which serves as the physical abode of the indwelling of the *Divine Presence on earth and as the venue for the sacrificial service. The Temple is destined to be the focal point of all spiritual consciousness. The first Temple was built by King Solomon (833 BCE) and destroyed by the Babylonians (423 BCE); the second Temple was built by Zerubabel (synonymous, according to some opinions, with Nehemiah, 353 BCE), remodeled by Herod and destroyed by the Romans (68 CE); the third, eternal Temple will be built by the *Messiah.

Tetragrammaton: see Names of God.

thanksgiving: see *sefirot*.

tikun ("rectification"): 1. A state of perfection and order. 2. "The world of *Tikun*" is the *world that first manifests this state, which is synonymous with the world of *Atzilut* (and *Berudim*, see Worlds). 3. The spiritual process of liberating the fragments of Divine light trapped within the material realm, unconscious of God's presence, thereby restoring the world to its initially intended state of perfection. This is accomplished through the performance of *mitzvot. 4. A remedy prescribed against the effects of committing a specific sin.

tikunei dikna: the 13 elements of the metaphoric beard of the *partzuf Arich Anpin, or the 9 such elements of the *partzuf Zeir Anpin.

tohu ("chaos"): 1. the primordial, unrectified state of creation. 2. "The world of *Tohu*" is the *world which manifests this state, synonymous with the initial, premature form of the world of *Atzilut*. It itself develops in two stages: a relatively stable form (*Akudim*) followed by an unstable form (*Nekudim*, see Worlds). The world of *Tohu* is characterized by great lights entering premature vessels, resulting in the breaking of the vessels. See also **tikun*.

Torah study: one of the 613 commandments. Considered the consummate commandment, equal in importance to all others.

Tree of Life: see *sefirot*.

trust: see *sefirot*.

truth: see *sefirot*.

tzadik (lit., "righteous" person; pl., *tzadikim*): one who has fully overcome the evil inclination of his animal soul (and converted its potential into good). See *beinoni*.

tzedakah: lit., "charity." Because of its importance, in Rabbinic literature it is referred to simply as "the commandment."

tzimtzum ("contraction"): the contraction and metaphoric removal of God's infinite light in order to allow for the creation of independent realities. The primordial **tzimtzum* produced the vacated space, devoid of direct awareness of God's Presence.

understanding: see *sefirot*.

yichud (lit., "unification"; pl., *yichudim*): a type of **tikun* in which one does not need to separate good from evil but rather focuses consciousness on the inherent spiritual unity between two apparently disparate concepts. See **birur*. 2. a specific spiritual exercise of this nature.

vav: a letter in the **Hebrew Alphabet.

victory: see *sefirot*.

will: see *sefirot*.

wisdom: see *sefirot*.

World to Come (*olam haba*, in Hebrew): the rectified state of eternal human existence, which follows the **Days of the Messiah and the resurrection of the dead.

World: a spiritual level of creation, representing a rung on the continuum of consciousness or awareness of God. In general, there are four worlds: *Atzilut*, *Beriah*, *Yetzirah*, and *Asiyah*. In particular, however, these four worlds originate from a fifth, higher world,

Adam Kadmon. All ten *sefirot and twelve *partzufim are manifest in each world; however, since there is a one-to-one correspondence between the worlds and the *sefirot,* a particular *sefirah* dominates in each world.

The world of *Atzilut* is fundamentally different from the three subsequent worlds in that in it there is no awareness of self *per se,* while the three lower worlds are progressive stages in the development of self-awareness.

The worlds correspond to God's essential Name *Havayah* and the *sefirot as follows:

letter of Havayah	world	dominant *sefirah*	level of consciousness
קוצו של י	אָדָם קַדְמוֹן Adam Kadmon Primordial Man	crown	Divine will to create and plan of creation
י	אֲצִילוּת Atzilut Emanation	wisdom	solely of God; no self-awareness
ה	בְּרִיאָה Beriah Creation	understanding	potential existence; formless substance
ו	יְצִירָה Yetzirah Formation	loving-kindness thru foundation	general existence: archetypes, species
ה	עֲשִׂיָּה Asiyah Action	kingdom	particular existence; individual creatures

In particular, the world of *Atzilut* develops out of *Adam Kadmon* in three stages (the names of which are taken from *Genesis* 30:10):

World		developmental stage	Description	
עֲקֻדִּים *Akudim*	"bound," "striped"	ten lights in one vessel	stable chaos	תֹּהוּ *Tohu*
נְקֻדִּים *Nekudim*	"dotted," "spotted"	ten lights in ten vessels, unstable	unstable chaos, collapse	
בְּרֻדִּים *Berudim*	"patterned," "speckled"	ten lights in ten inter-included vessels; stable	stable, mature rectification	תִּקּוּן *Tikun*

Whenever unqualified reference is made to the world of *Atzilut*, its final, mature stage is meant. It should be noted as well that our physical universe is *below* and enclothes the final two *sefirot* (foundation and kingdom) of the spiritual world of *Asiyah* referred to above.

Yetzirah: see Worlds.

Yom Kipur ("Day of Atonement"): the holiest day of the Jewish year, marked by fasting and a return to God, particularly through confession of sin.

yud: letter of the *Hebrew Alphabet.

Zeir Anpin: see *partzufim*.

Bibliography

Note: Words preceded by an asterisk have their own entries.

Biblical texts are cited by chapter and verse. If a post-Biblical text is divided into chapters, sections, or the like, it is cited accordingly. Otherwise, it is cited according to its pagination. There are two systems of pagination used in post-Biblical texts. The classic system is that of the Talmud, in which the page number refers to the physical page ("leaf" or "folio"), which is followed by a letter which refers to the column of the page. This usually means that column "a" is on the front side ("recto") of the page, and column "b" on the back ("verso"), but if there are two columns on a page, columns "a" and "b" will be on the front, and columns "c" and "d" on the back. This system was abandoned in later works, which are paginated in the modern fashion, each side of the page having its own number. In citations, then, "43c" means page 43, column 3 of a work paginated in the Talmudic fashion, and "p. 43" means simply page 43 of a work paginated in the modern fashion. References to Talmudic pagination are not preceded by "p.," since the letter following the number makes it clear that the reference is to a page and not a section. References to modern pagination, however, are preceded by "p." in order to distinguish them from references to sections.

Asarah Ma'amarot: ("Ten Articles"): Kabbalistic-philosophical work by Rabbi Menachem Azariah of Pano (1548-1620).

Avodah Zarah ("Idolatry"): tractate of the *Talmud.

Avot ("Fathers"): tractate of the *Talmud.

Bava Metzi'a ("The Middle Gate"): a tractate of the *Talmud.

Berachot ("Blessings"): tractate of the *Talmud.

Bereishit Rabah: the *Midrash to the book of *Genesis.

Bible: the written *Torah. The Bible comprises twenty-four books, divided into three sections: (1) the Torah ("teaching"), comprising the five books of Moses; (2) the eight books of the Prophets (the first and second books of Samuel and Kings are considered one book, as are the twelve "minor" prophets); (3) the eleven books of the Writings (the books of Ezra and Nehemiah are considered one book, as are the two books of Chronicles). The Bible is therefore known in Hebrew as the *Tanach*, the abbreviation formed by the first letters of the names of these three sections.

All the books of the Bible are authored by G-d, though transmitted through prophecy via the souls of the various prophets, who are known as the "authors" of the books themselves. Thus, every aspect of these texts contains infinite levels of meaning. If properly studied, they yield the profoundest insights available in any field of knowledge.

Although the division of the Bible into chapters and verses is of medieval, non-Jewish origin, its use has become standard in all Jewish books. The traditional division is into non-numbered paragraphs (*parashiot*, sing. *parashah*) and verses. In addition, the Torah is divided into 54 sections (also *parshiot*), at least one of which is read each week in the synagogue.

Bikurim ("First Fruits"): tractate of the *Talmud.

Body, Mind, and Soul: by Rabbi Yitzchak Ginsburgh on human physiology and medicine based on Kabbalah (published 2003).

Chagigah ("The Festival Offering"): tractate of the *Talmud.

Chronicles: book of the *Bible.

Chulin ("Profane [Food]"): tractate of the *Talmud.

Consciousness & Choice: by Rabbi Yitzchak Ginsburgh integrating modern decision theory as seen in Kabbalah and Chassidut with the search to find one's soul mate (published 2004).

Daniel: book of the *Bible.

Derech Chaim: volume of Chassidic teachings written by the second *Lubavitcher Rebbe, Rabbi Dov Ber Schneersohn (1773-1827) as a second part to his earlier volume titled *Sha'arei Teshuvah*.

Derech Mitzvotecha ("The Way of Your Commandments" [Psalms 119:32]): by the third Lubavitcher Rebbe, Rabbi Menachem Mendel of Lubavitch (1789-1866). Chassidic discourses. Paltova, 1911.

Deuteronomy: book of the *Bible.

Ein Yakov: anthology of all the homiletic material in the *Talmud. Compiled by Rabbi Ya'akov Ibn Chabib (1460-1516).

Eiruvin ("Mixing [Domains]"): tractate of the *Talmud.

Emunah Vemuda'oot ("Faith and Consciousness"): Hebrew volume by Rabbi Yitzchak Ginsburgh dealing with faith and its principles.

Exodus: book of the *Bible.

Genesis: book of the *Bible.

Gevurot Hashem: Medieval philosophical work on the Exodus by Rabbi Yehuda Loew of Prague (1512-1609).

Hagadah: the standardized liturgical program for the first eve of Passover.

Halachot Gedolot: ("Greater Halachot"): 8th century codex of Jewish law by Rabbi Shimon Kayra.

Hayom Yom: daily almanac for the year 5704 (1943-4) compiled by the Lubavitcher Rebbe, Rabbi Menachem Mendel Schneersohn.

Hilchot De'ot: section of Maimonides *Mishneh Torah*.

Hilchot Isurei Bi'ah: section of Maimonides *Mishneh Torah*.

Hilchot Ma'achalot Asurot: section of Maimonides *Mishneh Torah*.

Hilchot Melachim: section of Maimonides *Mishneh Torah*.

Hilchot Teshuvah: section of Maimonides *Mishneh Torah*.

Hilchot Yesodei Hatorah: section of Maimonides *Mishneh Torah*.

Ibn Ezra: grammatically oriented Medieval literal commentary of the Five Books of Moses by Rabbi Abraham Ibn Ezra (c.1089-1164).

Igeret HaKodesh ("The Holy Letter"): fourth section of the *Tanya* by Rabbi Shneur Zalman of Liadi (1745-1812).

Igrot Kodesh (Lubavitcher Rebbe): a compilation of the Lubavitcher Rebbe, Rabbi Menachem Mendel Schneersohn's, correspondence.

Isaiah: book of the *Bible.

Jerusalem Talmud: see Talmud.

Job: book of the *Bible.

Jonah: book of the *Bible.

Joshua: book of the *Bible.

Keter Shem Tov ("The Crown of Good Name" [*Avot* 4:13]): collection of Chassidic teachings of Rabbi Yisrael Ba'al Shem Tov (1698-1760) compiled by Rabbi Aharon of Opt. Zolkova, 1794. Cited according to the Kehot (NY, 1972) edition.

Ketubot ("Wedding Contracts"): tractate of the *Talmud.

Kidushin ("Betrothals"): tractate of the *Talmud.

Kings: book of the *Bible.

Lamentations: book of the *Bible.

Leviticus: book of the *Bible.

Likutei Moharan: collected Chassidic teachings of Rabbi Nachman of Breslov (1772-1810).

Likutei Tefilot: compilation of prayers based on Rabbi Nachman of Breslov's teachings (1772-1810).

Likutei Torah (Arizal's): collected teachings of the *Arizal* on the *Torah, edited by Rabbi Meir Popperos (1624-1662). Zalkova, 1775.

Makot: ("Lashes"): tractate of the *Talmud.

Malachi: book of the *Bible.

Ma'amarei Admor Hazaken ("Discourses of the Alter Rebbe"): series of Chassidic discourses from the founder of the Chabad Chassidic movement, Rabbi Shneur Zalman of Liadi (1745-1812). Published by year of original teaching (1802-1811), by books of the Bible, and by topic. New York: Kehot Publications Society.

Midrash (pl., Midrashim): the second major body of the oral Torah (after the *Talmud), consisting of Halachic or homiletic material couched as linguistic analyses of the Biblical text. An individual work of midrashic material is also called a Midrash; a specific analysis is called a midrash.

The Midrash is a corpus of many works written over the span of several centuries (roughly the second to the eighth CE), mostly in the Holy Land. The chief collection of homiletic midrashic material is the *Rabah* ("great") series, covering the five books of Moses and the five scrolls. Other important collections are *Midrash Tanchuma, *Midrash Lekach Tov on Tehilim, Pesikta d'Rav Kahana, *Pirkei d'Rabbi Eliezer* and *Tana d'bei Eliahu. Several later collections contain material that has reached us in its original form. These include *Midrash HaGadol* and *Yalkut Shimoni. There are many smaller, minor

Midrashim, as well; some of these are to be found in the collection *Otzar HaMidrashim*. Halachic Midrashim include the *Mechilta* (on Exodus), the *Sifra* (on Leviticus) and the *Sifrei* (on Numbers and Deuteronomy).

Midrash Bamidbar Rabah: see Midrash.

Midrash Shemot Rabah: see Midrash.

Midrash Shmuel Rabati: see Midrash.

Midrash Shocher Tov: see Midrash.

Midrash Tanchuma: see Midrash.

Midrash Vayikra Rabah: see Midrash.

Mishnah: see Talmud.

Nedarim ("Vows"): tractate of the *Talmud.

Numbers: book of the *Bible.

Ohalot: ("Tents"): tractate of the *Talmud.

Onkelos: see Targum.

Pardes Rimonim ("The Pomegranate Orchard"): the major work of Rabbi Moshe Cordovero (1522-1570).

Pri Aitz Chayim: ("The Fruit of the Tree of Life"). exposition of the liturgy based on the *Arizal's* writings. Koretz, 1785.

Prophets: see *Bible.

Proverbs: book of the *Bible.

Psalms: book of the *Bible.

Radak (Rabbi David Kimchi, 1160-1235): commentary on the *Bible. Cited according to Biblical passage discussed. Lemburg, 1868.

Ramban (Rabbi Moshe ben Nachman, 1194-1270): commentary on the Five Books of Moses. Cited according to Biblical passage discussed. Rome, before 1480.

Rashi (Rabbi Shlomo ben Yitzchak, 1040-1105): commentary on the Bible. Cited according to Biblical passage discussed. First printed in Italy, 1475.

Samuel: book of the *Bible.

Sanhedrin ("The Sanhedrin"): tractate of the *Talmud.

Sefer Hachinuch ("The Book of Education"): 13ᵗʰ century anonymously published text exhaustively listing and expounding on all 613 commandments of the *Torah.

Sefer Ha'ikarim ("The Book of Principles"): Medieval Jewish philosophical work by Rabbi Yosef Albo (c.1380-c.1444) that focuses primarily on the topic of principles of faith.

Sefer Hama'amarim 5666 ("The Book of Discourses 5766"): volume of Chassidic discourses by the fifth Lubavitcher Rebbe, Rabbi Shalom Dov Ber Schneersohn (1860-1920).

Sefer Yetzirah ("The Book of Formation"): fundamental text of Kabbalah, containing teachings that date back to Abraham, redacted by Rabbi Akiva (2ⁿᵈ century). Mantua, 1562.

Sha'ar Hapsukim ("Gate of Verses"): part of the *Eight Gates* series of teachings of the *Arizal, edited by Rabbi Shmuel Vital (?-1677). Jerusalem, 1868.

Shabbat ("The Sabbath"): tractate of the *Talmud.

Shekalim ("Coins"): tractate of the *Talmud.

Shemot Rabah: see Midrash.

Shocher Tov: see Midrash.

Shulchan Aruch ("The Set Table" [Ezekiel 23:41]): by Rabbi Yosef Karo (1488-1575). The Code of Jewish law. Cited by volume name (*Orach Chaim, Yoreh Deah, Even HaEzer,* and *Choshen Mishpat*), chapter, and paragraph. Venice, 1564.

Sifra Detzni'uta: see *Zohar*.

Sod Hashem Liyerei'av ("The Secret of God is to Those who Fear Him" [Psalms 25:14]): by Rabbi Yitzchak Ginsburgh. A Hebrew volume containing 50 meditations on God's essential Name, *Havayah*. Jerusalem: Gal Einai, 1985.

Sotah ("The Suspected Adulteress"): tractate of the *Talmud.

Ta'anit ("The Fast"): tractate of the *Talmud.

Talmud ("learning"): the written version of the greater part of the oral *Torah, comprising mostly legal but also much homiletic and even some explicitly mystical material.

The Talmud comprises the Mishnah ("repetition") and the *Gemara* (lit., "comprehension"). The Mishnah is the basic compendium of the laws (each known as a *mishnah*) comprising the oral Torah, redacted by Rabbi Yehudah the Prince in the second century CE. The Mishnah was elaborated upon over the next few centuries in the academies of the Holy Land and Babylonia; this material is the *Gemara*.

There are thus two Talmuds: the one composed in the Holy Land, known as the *Talmud Yerushalmi* ("The Jerusalem Talmud"), completed in the third century, and the one composed in Babylonia, known as the *Talmud Bavli* ("The Babylonian Talmud), completed in the sixth century.

The Mishnah—and *ipso facto* the Talmud—is divided into tractates. References to the Mishnah are simply the name of the tractate followed by the number of the chapter and individual *mishnah*. The Jerusalem Talmud was first printed in Venice, 1523-24. Although subsequent editions have generally followed the same pagination as this edition, it is nonetheless cited by chapter and *halachah* (i.e., individual *mishnah*) number, as is the Mishnah. References to it are therefore prefaced by "Y.," to distinguish them from references to the Mishnah itself. The Babylonian Talmud was first printed in its entirety in Venice, 1520-23, and subsequent editions have followed the same pagination as this edition, as well. References to the tractates of the *Talmud Bavli* are simply by tractate name followed by page and column ("a" or "b").

Talmudic Encyclopedia: monumental work, still in progress (26 vols. to date), aiming to present the entire Talmudic corpus in encyclopedic format. Begun in 1947, the project's first editor was Rabbi Shlomo Yosef Zevin.

Tana Debei Eliyahu: see Midrash.

Tanchuma: see Midrash.

Tanya ("It has been taught"): by Rabbi Shneur Zalman of Liadi (1745-1812). Seminal work of Chabad *Chassidut*. Also known as *Likutei Amarim* ("Collected Teachings") and *Sefer shel Beinonim* ("The Book of the *Beinonim*"). Slavita, 1796. English translation: New York: Kehot, 1962-69.

Targum: Translations of the Bible into *Aramaic. *Onkelos* (2nd century), a Roman convert to Judaism, translated the Five Books of Moses. *Yonatan* (ben Uziel, 1st century) translated the Five Books of Moses and the *Prophets. A collection of translations known as the *Yerushalmi* (Jerusalem) translations covers the entire *Bible.

The Art of Education: by Rabbi Yitzchak Ginsburgh. Published by Gal Einai, 2005.

The Hebrew Letters: by Rabbi Yitzchak Ginsburgh. Published also as *The Alef-Beit*. Jerusalem: Gal Einai, 1991.

The Mystery of Marriage: by Rabbi Yitzchak Ginsburgh. Published by Gal Einai, 1999.

Torah ("teaching"): God's will and wisdom as communicated to man. It pre-existed creation, and G-d used the Torah as His blueprint in creating the world.

God certainly communicated the teachings of the Torah in some form to Adam, who then transmitted them orally from generation to generation. However, God "officially" gave the Torah to mankind c. 1313 BCE (and during the ensuing 40 years) at Mt. Sinai through Moses. The Ten Commandments were pronounced in the presence of the entire Jewish people.

God gave the Torah in two parts: the written Torah and the oral Torah. The written Torah originally consisted of the Five Books of Moses (the "Pentateuch"), the other books being added later (see Bible). The oral Torah was communicated together with the Five Books of Moses as an explanation of the laws and lore included in it. This material was later written down by the sages of the oral Torah in the form of the *Talmud, the *Midrash, and the *Zohar. (All references to "the sages" in this book refer to the sages who transmitted the oral Torah as recorded in these works.)

Torah Or ("Torah Light" [Proverbs 6:23]): by Rabbi Shneur Zalman of Liadi (1745-1812). Chassidic discourses. Kapust, 1837.

Torah Temimah: ("Complete Torah" [based on Psalms 19:8]): Rabbi Baruch Halevi Epstein (1860-1942). commentary on the Five Books of Moses that integrates the Halachic and homiletic teachings of the sages.

Transforming Darkness into Light: by Rabbi Yitzchak Ginsburgh. Psychology and Kabbalah, published by Gal Einai, 2002.

Vayikra Rabah: see Midrash.

What You Need to Know About Kabbalah: by Rabbi Yitzchak Ginsburgh. A Basic through intermediate level introduction to Kabbalah, published by Gal Einai, 2006.

Writings: see Bible.

Yalkut Shimoni: see Midrash.

Yevamot ("Levirite Marriage"): tractate of the *Talmud.

Yoma ("The Day [of Atonement]"): tractate of the *Talmud.

Zachariah: book of the *Bible.

Zephaniah: book of the *Bible.

Zohar ("Brilliance"): by Rabbi Shimon bar Yochai (2nd century). One of the basic texts of the oral *Torah and *Kabbalah*. The Zoharic literature includes the *Zohar* proper, the **Tikunei Zohar*, and the **Zohar Chadash*. The *Zohar* was printed in 1558 in both Mantua and Cremona, but standard pagination follows the Mantua edition. The *Zohar* includes sections with specific titles, among them *Sifra Detzini'uta, Idra Raba, Idra Zuta, Midrash Hane'elam,* and *Ra'aya Mehemna*.

Subject Index

210

Proper Names Index

Gematria Index